Iaroslav Petik

Politics and Society in the Ukrainian People's Republic (1917–1921) and Contemporary Ukraine (2013–2022)
A Comparative Analysis

With a foreword by Mykola Doroshko

UKRAINIAN VOICES

Collected by Andreas Umland

45 Kateryna Pylypchuk
    The War that Changed Us
    Ukrainian Novellas, Poems, and Essays from 2022
    With a foreword by Victor Yushchenko
    ISBN 978-3-8382-1859-5

46 Kyrylo Tkachenko
    Rechte Tür Links
    Radikale Linke in Deutschland, die Revolution und der Krieg in der Ukraine, 2013-2018
    ISBN 978-3-8382-1711-6

47 Alexander Strashny
    The Ukrainian Mentality
    An Ethno-Psychological, Historical and Comparative Exploration
    With a foreword by Antonina Lovochkina
    Translated from the Ukrainian by Michael M. Naydan and Olha Tytarenko
    ISBN 978-3-8382-1886-1

48 Alona Shestopalova
    From Screens to Battlefields
    Tracing the Construction of Enemies on Russian Television
    ISBN 978-3-8382-1884-7

The book series "Ukrainian Voices" publishes English- and German-language monographs, edited volumes, document collections, and anthologies of articles authored and composed by Ukrainian politicians, intellectuals, activists, officials, researchers, and diplomats. The series' aim is to introduce Western and other audiences to Ukrainian explorations, deliberations and interpretations of historic and current, domestic, and international affairs. The purpose of these books is to make non-Ukrainian readers familiar with how some prominent Ukrainians approach, view and assess their country's development and position in the world. The series was founded, and the volumes are collected by Andreas Umland, Dr. phil. (FU Berlin), Ph. D. (Cambridge), Associate Professor of Politics at the Kyiv-Mohyla Academy and an Analyst in the Stockholm Centre for Eastern European Studies at the Swedish Institute of International Affairs.

Iaroslav Petik

POLITICS AND SOCIETY IN THE UKRAINIAN PEOPLE'S REPUBLIC (1917–1921) AND CONTEMPORARY UKRAINE (2013–2022)
A Comparative Analysis

With a foreword by Mykola Doroshko

Bibliografische Information der Deutschen Nationalbibliothek
Die Deutsche Nationalbibliothek verzeichnet diese Publikation in der Deutschen Nationalbibliografie; detaillierte bibliografische Daten sind im Internet über http://dnb.d-nb.de abrufbar.

Bibliographic information published by the Deutsche Nationalbibliothek
Die Deutsche Nationalbibliothek lists this publication in the Deutsche Nationalbibliografie; detailed bibliographic data are available in the Internet at http://dnb.d-nb.de.

Cover pictures:
https://de.wikipedia.org/wiki/Symon_Petljura#/media/Datei:Symon_Petlura._Photo_1920s.jpg
https://de.wikipedia.org/wiki/Wladimir_Iljitsch_Lenin#/media/Datei:Vladimir_Lenin.jpg
Photo 27183392 | Putin © Wrangel | Dreamstime.com
Photo 267698591 © Vitaliy Hrabar | Dreamstime.com

ISBN-13: 978-3-8382-1817-5
© *ibidem*-Verlag, Hannover • Stuttgart 2024
Alle Rechte vorbehalten

Das Werk einschließlich aller seiner Teile ist urheberrechtlich geschützt. Jede Verwertung außerhalb der engen Grenzen des Urheberrechtsgesetzes ist ohne Zustimmung des Verlages unzulässig und strafbar. Dies gilt insbesondere für Vervielfältigungen, Übersetzungen, Mikroverfilmungen und elektronische Speicherformen sowie die Einspeicherung und Verarbeitung in elektronischen Systemen.

All rights reserved. No part of this publication may be reproduced, stored in or introduced into a retrieval system, or transmitted, in any form, or by any means (electronic, mechanical, photocopying, recording or otherwise) without the prior written permission of the publisher. Any person who commits any unauthorized act in relation to this publication may be liable to criminal prosecution and civil claims for damages.

Printed in the EU

Contents

Foreword by *Mykola Doroshko* 7

1. The Idea of Analysis 9
2. The Political Events in the UPR and Contemporary Ukraine 27
3. Bolshevik Soviet Russia and Putin's Russia 65
4. Contemporary Ideological Debates 83
5. Major Shifts in Power 99
6. Diplomacy and International Relations 117
7. Military Campaigns 135
8. Ukrainian Society in 2014–22 and in 1917–22 153

Conclusion 171

Bibliography 189

Foreword

This book is a symbiosis of political philosophy, philosophy of history, and certain elements of actual history. It proposes to gain new perspectives on the current political situation in Ukraine, amidst Russia's unprovoked aggression, through analysis and comparison of past stages of the country's development.

The periods examined by the author are the era of the Ukrainian National Revolution (1917-1921) and the period of Ukraine's development after the Revolution of Dignity and before the full-scale Russian invasion (2013-2022). Various aspects of the politics of both periods are compared and studied throughout the text.

The author employs the philosophy of history by Wilhelm Dilthey, which emphasizes empathetic understanding and non-linear analysis, coupled with a psychological approach to understanding the role of specific historical figures. This allows for a deeper understanding of key events while still enabling the drawing of general conclusions.

Different chapters analyze and compare key aspects of the life of the Ukrainian state and the Eastern European region in general. However, the analysis goes beyond a simple comparison of details. Instead, the author classifies events and processes, seeking both similarities and differences to make the comparison more fruitful. Special attention is given to culture and society.

Military history, foreign policy, and domestic policy facts are also studied and analyzed. This book will be beneficial for those interested in Ukrainian politics, history, and the philosophy of history in general.

Mykola Doroshko,
Doctor of Historical Sciences,
Professor
Kyiv National University of Taras Shevchenko

1. The Idea of Analysis

Wilhelm Dilthey was a German philosopher who lived in the 19th century and the beginning of the 20th century. He was interested in hermeneutics and the methodology of science, but his most famous idea was his concept of the philosophy of history.

Prior to Dilthey, few philosophers had created original conceptions of the philosophy of history. The most popular such concept was probably that of G.W.F. Hegel, who speculated that the whole of human history is a development of the Absolute Idea. In this way, human history can be understood rationally through careful study of the meaning of each period in the general picture.

The great ancient Greek philosopher Aristotle started both the philosophy of history and political science by writing a book whence he argued that any state proceeds through a fixed cycle of a few periods—degrading from the Golden Age of the "enlightened aristocracy" to the horrors of the chaotic and corrupted "power of the crowd."

Scholastic and early patristic philosophers of the Middle Ages who wrote on the topic of politics and history mostly theorized about the connection of the divine and material worlds. St Augustine is considered the first scholar who thought of history as a linear development and not as a continuation of Aristotelian cycles. Most of the classic political philosophers and philosophers of history, however, have their roots in the works of Hegel, who was the first scholar to propose a rational view on the subject.

Dilthey's concept is completely different. Instead of the rational approach, Wilhelm Dilthey proposes something completely irrational—to try to understand history through empathy. Empathy is a method borrowed from psychology. It involves emotional, subjective involvement in an area that gives genuine intrinsic knowledge about it.

This method is incompatible with Hegel's rational idealistic philosophy as well as the political science method based on pure quantitative analytics. This does not mean, however, that it uses only subjective emotions or does not take facts into consideration.

On the contrary, particular facts about historical events are the starting point for empathetic understanding.

Empathetic "feeling" of the historical event helps to understand both its underlying mechanisms and its disposition toward contemporary history and events. In a sense, Dilthey theorized that past events are present in the contemporary epoch and by empathy we can understand not only the past but also the present and the future.

In this way, studying history is a hermeneutical search for special keys that open a deeper understanding of contemporary events. And that is the precise underlying idea of this book — to compare the past and the present to try to find new insights for actual problems.

Hermeneutics is a subdiscipline of continental philosophy devoted to the interpretation and understanding of texts and other symbol-based artifacts of human culture. Dilthey's philosophy of history is tightly connected to hermeneutics as he attributed a major role to symbol-based artifacts for understanding history.

The period of the few years leading up to 2022 is chosen because it is precisely the most contemporary time for Ukrainian political history. It is dramatic and includes a number of unsolved problems and conflicts. The beginning of the Russian invasion of Ukraine in February of 2022, however, marks the next period, which is not yet possible to assess.

It is nevertheless possible to give a certain prognosis of what will happen in the next era based on the empirical data of previous events. It involves more political analysis than historical work, but these two spheres often come as a pair.

Why compare the period of the Ukrainian People's Republic and the period between 2013 and 2022? These two periods have both astonishing similarities and deep differences. The UPR was one of the few times when the Ukrainian nation gained political autonomy and a separate state, a great achievement. The previous periods comprise the era of Bohdan Khmelnytsky and a few of his successors and (debatably) the medieval era of Kievan Rus'.

To clarify terms. In the period of the 1917--1922 on the territory of Ukraine, there were different political administrations. It was not called the UPR during the Skoropadsky period. The name was "Ukrainian state.". Some historians would prefer to refer toather call this period as the '"Ukrainian Revolution".

The next such period occurred only seven decades later with the crash of the Soviet Union and the establishment of a new Ukraine as an independent state. The events that have unfolded since 2013, however, show that there are many obstacles for the Ukrainian nation and that whether Ukraine will still hold its political independence remains a question. This makes this research even more important.

Why did the UPR eventually fail? What were our predecessors' right and wrong decisions? What was the geopolitical situation at that time? And what does this say about its contemporary counterpart?

In 2013 and 2014, the Revolution of Dignity in Ukraine caused the change of the government and the military annexation of Crimea by Russia as well as the start of the military conflict in the Donbass region of Ukraine. This event both raised the fervor of patriotism and the spirit of heroism among the Ukrainians and created a potential danger to the very existence of this independent nation.

Before February of 2022, Ukrainian society faced many challenges, problems, and unresolved internal conflicts. Nevertheless, it is hard to compare these problems to what followed with the full-scale Russian invasion. The bigger picture of Ukrainian politics changed dramatically, and the previous period is now history (albeit recent history). And it is important to assess these events historically and to learn the lessons of the past.

As we started from the philosophy of history, we should first define the methodology of the research. Why use Dilthey's concept instead of other, similar conceptions?

On the one hand, the global picture that we imagine when speaking about the political events in the two time periods seems to imply that the Absolute Idea conception is a more suitable candidate for the main methodological schema. Indeed, Hegel's idealistic philosophy of history often served as an ideological basis for political systems with a strict hierarchy, including authoritarian regimes.

It was Hegel's systematic view that inspired Karl Marx's materialistic picture of human history. And it was precisely that picture that guided Vladimir Lenin and his party comrades when starting the Russian Revolution. Putin's Russia is evidently an authoritarian regime that seems even to be evolving into Soviet-like totalitarianism.

There is a famous historical anecdote that is hard to verify but very symptomatic of Hegel's worldview. It says that when Napoleon entered the city where the German philosopher lived at the time, Hegel praised him and said that the French conqueror was the "embodiment of an Absolute Idea."

Does the system's structure of the political theory presuppose authoritarian political structure as the foundation of its subject? The UPRR had many problems, but it cannot be called a purely authoritarian police state, especially when compared to the Bolshevik project. It is unlikely to be a suitable subject for a political theory that presupposes authoritarian social structure.

On the other hand, there are reasons to use empathetic understanding instead of only Hegel's method here. It is a question of the difference between a democracy and an authoritarian regime. The UPR is also probably a state that gives a much greater role to individual personalities and actions. In this way, a psychological concept of philosophy of history seems like a much more flexible option here.

Putin's Russia, however, is far closer to Hegel's ideas about a systematic and leader-centered political regime. In fact, contemporary Russian propaganda strives to present Vladimir Putin as a modern Napoleon. This brings all sorts of horrors connected to the imperialistic ambitions of the political leader, including war, but it is still an interesting case for political and historical analysis.

Apart from his main scientific activity, Dilthey was also a biographer who explored the lives of famous personalities. His biography of the philosopher Hegel studies the life of a great German idealist and how it influenced his own intellectual creativity.

Wilhelm Dilthey studies the people surrounding young Hegel, the culture of his time, his letters, and his intellectual projects. Dilthey then makes assumptions about how all of these little details defined the books of the German idealist and how his intellectual endeavors influenced the history of the society.

All these details are known as microhistory, the stories of separate personalities and families, as opposed to macrohistory, the stories of big movements, states, wars, and conflicts. For obvious reasons, the empathetic understanding of history is more grounded in microhistory. We try to understand particular personalities through the documents or interviews with witnesses, etc.

In this way, the idea of an empathetic understanding proposes to analyze the separate episodes rather than starting from a bigger, systematic picture. Nevertheless, it does not mean that this method is unsystematic—Dilthey still draws global conclusions and describes the epoch in general. Macrohistory can still be understood better through specific, minor details.

Consequently, this book will start by picking over each particular episode of the history of both periods to draw analogies and provide analysis. The bigger picture and the general context will be discussed later and in the light of the previously investigated details.

The book is devoted mostly to politics, and the table of contents lists chapters devoted to the different aspects of the life of the society of two periods. While there is a lot for a historian to study in the military history as well as the society of the UPR, politics remains the central term and topic. Why is that so?

Politics and policy encompass these different aspects and allow us to draw conclusions about the historical period in general. It also resonates with the proclaimed aim of the research: most of the actual problems of today's Ukrainian society concern politics or are at least connected to it.

Military, diplomatic, and sociological aspects are important for an understanding of the political situation. It is hard, however, to imagine the description of these particular aspects in isolation from the central term.

An empathetic understanding of history presupposes the analysis not only of the particular events and social groups, but also of the particular personalities and their biographies in the context of and in connection to the epoch. How can this part of the work be presented?

The UPR period was rich in strong and interesting personalities. The events of the Revolution brought many new people who could earn their new place only through talent and brave action to a previously closed and guarded political world. Some of these newcomers were intellectuals. Others were military-affiliated or even representatives of the lower social class. There were, of course, total failures, but all in all there are plenty of individuals who left their legacy in the history of the nation.

For contemporary Ukraine, the problem is far more complicated. There are many new faces in Ukrainian politics since 2013, and they also came up via the "social elevator" of the Revolution of Dignity and following military conflict. We cannot, however, assess their personalities the same way we assess historical figures. Most of the contemporary "newcomers" are still alive and active. There is no "historical horizon" between us and them that will allow for objective judgment.

There are interesting and strong-willed people among them too, of course. Our personal political affiliations and opinions, however, may cloud our judgment and be adding significantly to the simple "absence of horizon." What is more, the biographical analysis should employ a justified methodology.

Simple searching for similarities and differences is not enough. Empathetic understanding presupposes a big role for the particular personality in the historical process. Hegel's rational philosophy of history thinks in global variables and social systems, whereas Dilthey concentrates on the particular events and personalities.

Nevertheless, there is room to compare the intellectual biographies in this theory. Details about the life of an important political figure, especially the texts they read and other figures with whom they communicated, may be first incorporated into the picture of the period and their course of actions. Environment forms an agent, but after the formation is complete, the agent starts to change the environment.

In this way, empathetic understanding goes from the particular details to the epoch and back to particular details — working both with macrohistory and microhistory. This perfectly fits the scope of this work.

There was a lot of theory, and it should be illustrated with some examples. Let us assume that we are viewing the biography of an important diplomat X of the UPR period. We know that X worked in a particular sphere and influenced international relations in a particular way. We study the intellectual biography of X, including his education, network of contacts, and written documents. We make an assumption that the socialistic works that he studied at university defined his political affiliation and some of his main actions during the peak of his career.

These actions had consequences on the bigger picture. As X was an important figure, his actions profoundly influenced the international relations of the UPR. We have already established our theory about the initial role of socialist literature. We then proceed by placing the role of X in international relations into an even more general picture of the UPR's big politics.

X's actions were professional, but they were not aimed at the nationalistic ideology vector. Instead, his course of action was to reconnect with Soviet Russia even in times of a crisis in relations between the two countries. Maybe he was not a straightforward traitor but rather the passive supporter of some other ideology than nationalism.

We also should be historians and not the supporters of this or that ideology. It is true that in the contemporary situation, the author as a citizen of Ukraine is a supporter of this country and the pro-European vector of development, but this should not be an obstacle to objective assessment of historical events and the conflicting ideologies.

It is even more important for the UPR period as it is definitely pure history that should be assessed professionally. It is evident that pro-Soviet ideology and people like X played a negative role for the country's national culture and politics, including the consequences that are still present in Ukrainian society now. There is, however, no place for emotions.

X's status as only a passive supporter and not a direct adversary is also important. Was he afraid of persecution? Did he maybe not understand all the consequences of his actions at that time? These are also important things to understand about this personality and important details for an analysis of his actions in the scope of the general picture.

The process is simplified for the sake of example. It is doubtful that reading socialist literature alone would justify the complete career and key decisions of a political figure. The analysis, however, was guided by an empathetic understanding—we have tried to understand the objective diplomatic decisions through the details of an intellectual biography that are purely subjective. This analysis tries to understand the course of events by putting the researcher in the place of one of the agents who guided that course of events, by feeling and thinking like this agent, to a certain extent. That is a methodology of empathetic understanding.

The next phase is making general assumptions about the course of events in international relations during the UPR period and comparing them to international relations in a chosen contemporary period. Let us assume that the pro-socialist position of X was precisely why X and some of his colleagues were reluctant to support the nation-centered program of actions. This did not result instantly in the failure of international policy, but it was one of the complex of reasons for the downfall of the UPR.

We then state that international relations and diplomacy in contemporary Ukraine are still among the most important factors of politics, and there are different factions among Ukrainian diplomats as well. Empathetic understanding should not be understood as straightforwardly primitive. The researcher should not try to find the contemporary socialist who sabotaged the diplomatic process.

Nevertheless, we should concentrate on the contradictions among the diplomatic specialists in the UPR period. What were the reasons and consequences? What alternative decision could have been made? The existence of similar contradictions in contemporary history is already established. Of course, there will be a different set of reasons and consequences for those of today. But not completely different.

Some of the key contradictions, like pro-Russian and pro-Soviet ideology, still exist. In the case of X, he was a sympathizer of Soviet Russia for ideological reasons (i.e., reading socialist literature). It is doubtful that the same socialism literature would play the same role today. Nevertheless, these ideologies are still here, and they still can gain supporters through other media. They are transformed, and this makes the project of explaining this transformation from its roots even more interesting. But it is not a primitive analogy between two different events.

First of all, these events are connected, and they should be assessed genetically. There is an initial starting phase, significant details during the UPR period, and the continuing development through the next decades with an emergence in new form for contemporary Ukrainian society. This is the same as with macrohistory and microhistory: two different periods on the timeline complete each other, providing "keys" for each other. This goes perfectly well with Dilthey's empathetic understanding of history.

We cannot just find the contemporary counterpart Y who is also into socialism with all the following consequences. Most likely, we would say that X was a representative of a social group with a certain background, and that background for many historical reasons is still present in today's world albeit in a form that is a little bit changed. What is more, there are some diplomatic figures in contemporary Ukraine who may share that background.

By analyzing that background within its historical evolution, we will make an interesting case for comparative historical studies. That background is part of the historical circumstances of the epoch, and we reach the goal of the research by shifting from one period to another.

Empathetic understanding that concerns particular individuals is more or less intuitive because we try to understand others the same way in our daily life. But what does an empathetic understanding of abstract entities and events look like? What does it mean to have a genuine "feeling" of the event?

There is definitely a subtle process of hermeneutical decoding for a historian involved in microhistory. Studying the archives and artifacts that belonged to particular personalities and families inevitably involves scholars psychologically with the personalities and their stories.

These involvements include the empathetic understanding of the events that are part of the personality's story. Let us assume the historian X is studying a certain family of important public figures who lived a century ago. This family fell victim to political persecutions in the 1920s and 1930s, and an understanding of the persecution system of the period as well as the particular persecutions is vital to understanding the story of that family and continuing the research.

How is that possible? There are no such persecutions today, or persecutions in general take completely different forms. The idea is that by empathetically studying particular personalities and their life stories, the scholar becomes engaged in the life of the time period and the atmosphere of the society, including such events as the aforementioned political persecutions.

The scholar starts to understand those events through the guidance of the particular personalities. And just as Wilhelm Dilthey assumes this scholar starts to find "keys" for the contemporary world in past events, so too do they start to see their own reality differently than a non-educated individual.

That is the main advantage of studying history according to Dilthey, and it is the same with most of the humanities. Humanities are mostly studying different texts and artifacts created by humans. The main aim of this study, although it is sometimes not understood by all the participants of the process, is to understand humanity and human society better. Such a view is typical of a continental philosopher engaged in hermeneutics.

Hegel and his philosophy of history take a completely different approach. His hierarchical system does not take particular personalities and events into consideration. What is important for Hegel are structures and complex, long periods of time. Even such personalities as Napoleon are just a medium for general historical laws that are projected into reality. Not a person, but a nation. Not an individual, but a society. Not a state, but an empire. And so on.

Military events and battles are a completely separate sphere. Without a military education, it is possible to assess mostly the political side of each episode by centering on the media and the ideological consequences of the tragic events in both conflicts.

There are some central points in each period that are in a certain way "seductive" to compare. These "pairs" include the Battle of Kruty (1918) and the Ilovaysk Battle (2014), for example. Both were actual defeats of the Ukrainian Armed Forces, and both were the topics of heated ideological debates.

The Battle of Kruty happened during the Bolshevik offensive on Kyiv. Hundreds of young Ukrainian patriots, most of whom were students with no military experience or education (and some were even gymnastics students) marched to the Kruty railway station to meet the Russian army. Partially because of the difference in numbers (the Bolsheviks had a few thousand battle-hardened soldiers at their command) and partially because of some serious misguidance from their officers (also a topic for heated ideological debates), almost all the Ukrainian participants in the battle were slaughtered.

Ukrainians who fought and died at that battle are considered national heroes, whereas the Bolshevik army troops are condemned as war criminals. The pro-Soviet position is that although they were young, they were still soldiers (i.e., combatants). They were misguided by their officers and political leaders, but the Red Army commanders had no other choice than to face them in combat.

Counter arguments from pro-Soviet debaters include that one of the reasons no Ukrainian reinforcement was sent to Kruty was that at the same time a massive rebellion was started at the "Arsenal" factory in Kyiv. The rebellion was led by pro-Bolshevik proletarians and suppressed by pro-Ukrainian military forces. The ideology behind this counterargument is that despite the tragedy of the Battle of Kruty, pro-Ukrainian debate participants do not admit the tragedy of the opposing side.

The Ilovaysk Battle happened in August of 2014 in the Donbass region. It was part of the Anti-Terrorist Operation of the Ukrainian special services, police, and army against pro-Russian separatists. Before August, Ukrainian armed forces had managed to achieve serious successes, like defeating separatists at Slovyansk, and High Command planned to finish off the insurgents in just a few months. There were, however, experts who called for more caution lest a further offensive by the Russian Army from its borders create a so-called boiler.

A boiler is military-slang for the strategic situation when an opposing force surrounds the group of its adversaries and cuts off both supplies and communications. The surrounded group is a helpless target for artillery and without supplies or reinforcements is either slaughtered or taken as POWs.

Everything happened just as those experts predicted. Large Russian military forces invaded the region and surrounded Ukrainian battalions thereby blocking them in Ilovaysk. Ukrainian debaters state that those were regiments of the professional Russian Army, superior to opposing forces both in numbers and equipment. Separatists claim that those forces were comprised only partially of Russians who later legalized themselves as volunteers for the Luhansk People's Republic (LPR) and Donetsk People's Republic (DPR). This remains a topic for strong debate.

After several days of fierce combat, the Ukrainians decided to retreat. The negotiations were problematic for both sides and ended in tragedy for Ukrainian forces. Ukrainians asked for a safe humanitarian corridor. What happened next is difficult to establish precisely. Ukraine claims that the Russians deceived our side so as to commit what would later be called the Ilovaysk Massacre. When Ukrainian soldiers started to retreat, separatists opened fire, killing a few hundred and causing one of the highest casualty rates for the Ukrainian side for the whole campaign.

For their part, Russians claim that negotiations never ended in a decision. Some experts state that the corridor was opened for people only (i.e., with no weapons or vehicles), and some state that even that variant was not negotiated. Again, a very hot topic for debate.

As with all such debates, it is very hard to assess rationally. Too many extremely strong emotions are involved. And there are no "recipes." This, however, is exactly why political science and history of ideologies exist and why empathetic understanding is probably the only effective methodology here.

Pro-Russian and pro-Soviet journalists and historians, on the one hand, claim that these are precedents that prove the superiority of the invaders' planning, military command, and fighting spirit. Ukrainians, on the other hand, admit the mistakes in planning while emphasizing the heroism of ordinary soldiers and their sacrifice.

But are these two events even comparable? Is that comparative analysis justified? The general political context of the two battles differs greatly. And the particular military maneuvers are different not only due to battlefield differences, but also due to differences in historical periods and the military technologies involved.

What creates a "family resemblance" between two events is more ideological than purely military or political. There was a mistake in the planning of an operation. There were sacrifices made for that by simple soldiers. There is a great ideological significance to that event in Ukrainian society.

An investigation was launched concerning the tragedy of the Ilovaysk Battle. It never delivered any results. As for the Kruty Battle, due to the rapid development of further events, the only investigation that can be done now is by historians. The sacrifice of young lives that was made at that tragic event is sacred for Ukraine, and it makes the analysis even more complicated.

There are also other factors involved that make plain comparison of the events problematic. For example, in ATO/JFO, there was another event that is reminiscent of the Kruty Battle — the Debaltseve Battle. Then the Ukrainian forces also retreated and suffered casualties, and mistakes in planning were still present. Does that mean we should make the second analogy and compare three battles instead of two? Or should we concentrate on the global strategic situation instead? Or should we completely withdraw such comparison in principle?

So, what is the right approach when analyzing these and other military events of the two campaigns? The answer is just as for the case of diplomat X—analyzing the background rather than concentrating on the particular "family resemblance." The particular timeline with the key points of each period should be presented, but the analysis should refer to the ideology and background more than to the particular details.

The term "family resemblance," despite its somewhat ironic connotations, is quite a good term for the described situation. It comes from mathematics, where it is used to compare different mathematical structures, like separate algebraic formulas, groups, rings, and so on. Particular operations and nodes of the structure differ drastically, but when you view the structure in a more abstract way, you can see that the structures in general resemble each other. What is more, they sometimes descend from a common source and form a separate class, a "family."

Does the "family resemblance" between both the military and political events in two wars mean that history is repeating itself? From a historian's view, this problem concerns the aforementioned conception of the philosophy of history proposed by Aristotle. If there are precise event cycles in the politics of the country, then there is a possibility that there are event cycles in the military history of such a region as Eastern Europe. If this is the case, then the conflict between Ukraine and Russia makes up the next phase of the cycle because the lessons of the previous phase were not learned and the contemporary leaders will make the same mistakes that will cause more or less the same tragic consequences.

But what about not only progress in technology and sociopolitical organization, but also different geopolitical circumstances? Is the idea of cyclic development of history even rational? It was widely believed in Antiquity, but since the 19th century, the idea of progress in history prevails.

The circulated anecdote-like answer to this and similar questions is that history is more Vico's "infinite regress" than a circle, thereby implying it repeats itself but progresses toward some distant point on a linear scale as well. This is a sarcastic comment on the situation, but it bears some truth.

If there is a cyclic structure to history as an entity, it is more complex than a repeating circle of events and coexists with linear progressive development. The very idea of comparing the events at the center of the book is implying a certain cyclic structure, but it is not an Aristotelian variant or at least not only Aristotelian.

Returning to the "family resemblance" — it seems to be a far more fitting concept. Events of the two periods resemble each other but not completely. This fact is a reason to dig deeper and analyze the general background of the periods, which is a common approach for comparative studies.

In this way, it becomes even clearer that society and politics should be in the center of the view because they encompass the background of military and historical events. Dilthey sometimes refers to the concept of the "Zeitgeist," or the Spirit of the Time, which is a general pattern in the social and economic organization of the period that is also characterizing it in a subtle, existential way. Every epoch has a subtle aesthetic feeling for the one living in it.

There are definitely subtle and complex feelings best described by poetry and/or art of what it is to live through this particular day as an individual. How is this different from the Spirit of Time then? Is this Spirit just a sum of the poetic "feelings of time?"

Existential philosophy tends to explore that aspect of human life, centering also on the negative feelings connected to making decisions, etc. This is a type of philosophy genetically connected to hermeneutics, but it is very far from the philosophy of history. Spirit of Time is about an epoch, a big time period, and the social structures that form identity.

There is no room for the existential analysis of the period in the works devoted to comparative studies in history/politics. The Spirit of Time for the individual in the first sense presupposes subtle and deep feelings connected to philosophical aesthetics. As such, it is a natural companion to hermeneutics and empathy understood in a narrow sense. There is a second sense, however, which also was outlined by Dilthey.

Zeitgeist of the epoch is a vital part of the background and is important for the comparative study of the two time periods. The UPR is different from contemporary Ukraine because of not only the difference in technology and political circumstances, but also the difference in Spirit. Why that is so is a question for hermeneutics, but all in all, it is an established fact. The Spirit of Time in the second sense also presupposes certain empirical verification.

When we theorize about different epochs, we may say that this thing is hard to imagine happening in this epoch, whereas it was common in the second and vice versa. While it bears some spiritual component, most such instances arise for purely empirical reasons—the aforementioned technological and sociopolitical progress.

It was impossible for the UPR to hold against so many enemies in late 1919 and 1920, and this situation was caused by the geopolitics after the First World War. The geopolitical situation from 2013 to 2022 was completely different, so there is still a chance that it will worsen (from the Ukrainian point of view). This situation is part of the empirical data about the epochs, and it is empirically verified. Thus, Dilthey's second sense of the Zeitgeist is quite a good candidate for research here.

The geopolitical state of affairs in both of the time periods is probably the most complex topic that will be in the scope of this work. Intrinsically connected to the internal politics of the UPR and contemporary Ukraine, geopolitics requires deep knowledge of the history of the region and analytical skills to assess the situation of the planet and its connection to Eastern Europe.

Just to talk about the UPR period, you need to take the First World War into consideration, which involves the diplomatic and military history of Europe in the 19th century, and both Revolutions in Russia, which involves both the economic and social history of the Russian Empire in that period. You also need to know how to connect them to the local problems in the UPR and its influence on its neighbors. And it is not only about White Guard and Soviet Russia—Poland, Antanta, and German military forces and their interests should be taken into account as well.

As for contemporary Ukraine, the story of the late Soviet Union and post-Soviet period in Eastern Europe is extremely important. You cannot understand Vladimir Putin's ambitions without an analysis of the shift from the Soviet Union to contemporary Russia and its social, economic, and political results.

Were the annexation of Crimea and the war in Donbass good decisions even from the Russian pro-imperial point of view? Does it mean that the next phase of war will be successful for Russia or that Putin will be stopped? What are the lessons for Ukraine in this situation? How is the whole situation connected to its historical roots in the UPR period?

In this way, the research starts to concern comparative political science much more than just pure history. The project of the book assumes its main aim is not only a historical survey or philosophy of history practical drill, but also political science and contemporary policy-making analytics.

The last, but not least, aspect that should be considered is the society of both periods. As in the case of Zeitgeist, it is hard to provide an analysis of this aspect and stay neutral without dwelling in subjectivity. What was society during the UPR period like? We can only use empathy to understand the documents and artifacts of the epoch.

There are also some quantitative sociological parameters that should be compared (with empathy serving still as a guiding idea). Economically, contemporary Ukraine differs from the UPR greatly. Even if we do not take technological development into consideration, the proletarians in modern times are in completely different situations. The same applies for small farmers, etc. Yet there are still unsolved, old problems like poverty and quality of education.

War influences the state in both periods greatly—it consumes resources; creates additional, virulent corruption; and brings all sorts of internal conflicts inside the social structure. Nevertheless, as was outlined previously, the military conflicts of the UPR and contemporary Ukraine also differ greatly such that the quantitative sociological parameters should be analyzed accordingly and general consequences of the policy drawn.

Dilthey's hermeneutical method claims that it is enough. There is actually no other logical way to study the epoch than through the written documents. Critics might say that even the best scholar may be subjective here, but it seems that this is just the way historical research is at its core.

As for contemporary Ukraine—we are the witnesses of this epoch. Yet we are still subjective. Is the objective "feeling" of the epoch just some of those "subjective feelings?" Again, this is a question that mostly concerns hermeneutics as a subdiscipline more than philosophy of history. There is a particular representation of the individual's thoughts about an epoch, and given that the individual is rational, it is enough for historical analysis. This is the way the humanities, in general, work.

The author hopes that the reader will enjoy this essay-like historical/political book based on the outlined methodology.

2. The Political Events in the UPR and Contemporary Ukraine

Understanding the general timeline of the two periods as well as the geopolitical context is important for this research project. The chapter will not dwell on ancient history too much, but it will discuss the context of 19th-century Ukraine as well as the period after 1991 in the country.

At the end of the 19th century, the territory of Ukraine was incorporated into two giant Empires—the Austro-Hungarian Empire and the Russian Empire. The eastern and central parts of the country were under Russian rule, whereas the western part, including today's city of Lviv, was under Habsburg rule.

These two empires were rivals in the great geopolitical game. Nevertheless, they were connected by numerous complex economic relations. Ukrainians (or Rusini, as they were called at that time) inhabited both parts of the country. Most were peasants, whereas the cities were inhabited mostly by representatives of other nations (Russians, Poles, Jews, and German colonists).

Rusini were mostly uneducated and engaged in heavy physical labor most of their lives. The only social group that could allow for an education and work in the sphere of culture were village priests, who defined the tight connection between Ukrainian national culture of the period and religion.

The Rusini language (i.e., Ukrainian) was condemned as a dialect of the Russian language "spoiled" by Polish influence. A similar attitude was expressed by Austro-Hungarian officials. In the latter case, matters were complicated by the national politics of the Habsburg empire.

If in the Russian part of the country, the only problem was with the Russians as the metropole's nationality, in the Austro-Hungarian Empire that encompassed different nations, the relations between them and Rusini were quite tense. Poles, for example, who had more educated people among them, dominated in the field of politics with all the economic and cultural consequences for Rusini, who were practically absent in the political life of the country. While some of the aristocrats dwelled in the local culture in the Russian part of the country, the western part of the country had a mixed national question and socioeconomic tensions.

The language debate remains a very hot topic in contemporary Ukraine as well. People with pro-Russian positions tend to claim that the whole Ukrainian language is an artificial construct—clumsy, unnatural, and inapplicable to science or high poetry. It is merely a dialect for simple people who inhabit mostly villages and small provincial towns. The language for true intellectuals is Russian and Russian only.

Ukrainian intellectuals, for their part, claim that the language is a vital part of the national identity and those who criticize it do so due to their imperialistic ideology. You can easily claim that the territory ought to be colonized by you if the inhabitants of the territory do not have their own identity (of which language is an important part). The Ukrainian language and national culture are at the heart of many heated debates, including the actual ones.

Sometimes pro-Russian debaters refer to a sort of conspiracy theory about the Ukrainian language and the whole nation. It is speculated that it was German Chancellor Otto Bismarck's plan to weaken Russia both as a state and a nation by creating a "puppet ethnos" from the inhabitants of the southwestern parts of the empire.

This plan included creating the artificial language and spreading and developing it with the tools of secret diplomacy. Thus, a new national identity would be created within the borders of the Russian Empire that would inevitably bring conflict and separatism in the future. A similar role as a "puppet ethnos" is given to Belarusians that also has its consequences for national politics in Belarussia today.

Any sane historian will say that it is impossible to do so and that it is an awful example of chauvinist propaganda aligned with "The Protocols of the Elders of Zion" and "Dulles' Plan." Nevertheless, just as with these two documents, "Bismarck's project" remains a powerful tool of anti-Ukrainian propaganda.

In the UPR period, the "plan" had its "implications" as the UPR made a diplomatic agreement with the Reich to stop the war on this front and was later strongly supported by the German military in exchange for supplying resources to the Germans. Pro-Russian historians made a famous statement—"Ukraine as a separate nation was created in the German's Army General Headquarters."

It needs to be emphasized that although the First World War is not such a sacred object in today's Russia as the Second World War is, it is still an important period of national history. It is viewed as the grandiose clash of the civilizations. This was a total war: the battle of one type of values against the different types of values. Choosing a side in this clash is more than just fighting for resources. It is also a moral choice in the eyes of Russians. Thus, Ukrainians are condemned as traitors in this period as well.

That sounds very offensive to anyone who identifies themselves as a Ukrainian. Nowadays, Germany is just one of the representatives of the European Union, and the role of the "puppet master" in pro-Russian propaganda is given to the United States of America. It is stated that the European Union is just a proxy, a controlled structure, and the USA realizes its politics through this proxy. The Archenemy remains the same though—Western values, the Western World, and its influence.

Though tsarist Russia and Soviet Russia are strong ideological opponents, they were similar in their negation of everything that is connected to that influence. The tsarist regime provided censorship and political persecutions of Ukrainian culture. Ukrainian books were prohibited, so too were theater plays and any research into national history. Ukraine was considered a proxy for the Western World even at that time.

This had not only political consequences, but also an influence on a certain picture of Ukrainian culture. Russia's claim is that it is artificial, the same as the language, and is financed and developed only as a means for geopolitical manipulation. Any representative of national culture should not only create high-quality content, but also protect himself against these and similar accusations.

In these circumstances, people who are involved in Ukrainian culture play a political role as well. Nevertheless, this statement is not only true about the present day. Historically, the most famous and discussed "Ukrainian figure" is Taras Shevchenko, who was a poet and an artist. His works are the most cited among Ukrainian intellectuals, including in political contexts. Shevchenko, who wrote poems on political topics and the Ukrainian national movement, is viewed more as a prophet figure for the nation. It is important that this poet is a main symbol for the national idea, whereas most nations have instead military and political leaders in this role.

Thus, cultural activity, especially anything connected to developing the Ukrainian language, is viewed as political or even identified as a purely political activity. Many of the UPR's public figures or government officials came from the sphere of culture or even continued to work in that sphere in tandem with their main political activity. The "cultural horizon" as well as the "question of language" were extremely important for the politics of that period.

You can find dozens of points in Ukrainian history (including ancient) that are the topic of debates between people of pro-Russian and pro-Ukrainian positions. Discussions reach their peak when the events of the Second World War are raised. And it is important to know all the details to understand the discussion in general. We will just outline the main ones.

The first is the very origin of the Ukrainian nation. Was Kievan Rus' the ancestor of Ukraine or were Ukrainians "invented" in the modern times for the purpose of political manipulation? Were the Moscow-related princes corrupted by the influence of Asia? Was the western part of the country already inclined toward Europe at that time, and if so, what about the central and the eastern parts?

The short period of independence during and after Bohdan Khmelnytsky is a hot topic as well. Was Khmelnytsky the first representative of a separate Ukrainian political class or was he a Pole who rebelled against the king due to personal reasons and political ambitions? Was his union with Russia a good decision, and if so, does it mean he had an initial anti-European course? Was the failure of the next Hetmans to establish political stability an indication of Russian dominance in the region?

Ivan Mazepa and his relation to the Russian Empire should be mentioned as well. Mazepa was a hetman ruler of Ukraine after it was incorporated into the Russian Empire. He was a close friend and associate of the Russian emperor Peter the Great, but he had ambitions to rule the bigger region separately. Mazepa joined forces with the Swedish Empire in a war with Russia; he lost and died in exile.

It is important to mention this Hetman because this was the first time that the pro-Ukrainian political position was condemned as treason and a sort of moral crime by Russian officials and society. Since the Second World War, a radical Ukrainian nationalist is negatively associated with Stepan Bandera and is depicted as a supporter of a fascist regime, but in the time of the UPR and prior, it was the similar case with Mazepa.

Mazepa, just like Bandera, is condemned as an immoral criminal, and this detail is important to describe Russian ideology and propaganda even in today's world. In this worldview, the question of the separate development of the Ukraine as a nation is not even posed. Ukrainians are part of the Russian people — that is an axiom. And the betrayal of Mazepa is a betrayal of his own brother. There were even religious rituals involved in the official condemnation of the hetman in the Russian state.

Of course this is an example of virulent propaganda. There is no way a sane historian or culture studies scholar can deny the existence of a national culture of 30–35 million people and a few centuries of history comprising hundreds of poets, writers, scientists, etc. And as for the political decisions of the hetmans — that is all part of the political game and cannot be assessed in terms of moral obligations. The case is more complex in the context of the Second World War and collaboration with Nazism, but it is doubtful that the objective truth about those events is described by Russian propaganda either.

In this way, in the period preceding the UPR, Ukraine was divided between West and Asia not only in a political sense but also in a spiritual sense. This issue is also relevant for Ukraine in 2013-22. The eastern part of the country is influenced by Russia, Russian culture, and Russian language, whereas the western part of the country is influenced by European values and culture.

This "great division" is evident to anyone involved in the Ukrainian context both from the historical perspective and nowadays. This fact causes Ukraine to be the battlefield, not for different empires, but for the different types of civilization—the West and the East. This has its implications for both the UPR period and contemporary Ukraine.

Returning to the period preceding the UPR, the tensions between different political factions on both sides of the border were already quite serious. The Ukrainian national movement was slowly growing and gaining supporters as well as new ideas. Ukrainians from both the Russian Empire and Austria-Hungary created connections and dreamed of a unified Ukraine.

Unfortunately for the Ukrainian patriots at that time, there were misunderstandings and conflicts in the movement already, which grew with the movement. And this also had its consequences for the UPR period, of course. Western Ukrainians and the patriots from the eastern part of the country, although both hoping for the unification of the nation, had absolutely different pictures of how it would happen and, what is more important, who would be the leader of that unification.

The question of political independence was sort of taboo, however. It would bring additional suspicion toward the Ukrainian movement from government officials and seemed like something distant and unrealistic. There were some radicals, but most of the representatives of the movement had a limited autonomy as their biggest ambition. The idea of complete independence was formed among the radical minority much later.

The secret services of both the Austro-Hungarian Empire and the Russian Empire were rivals who were unified in their persecution of the participants of the Ukrainian national movement. You can find the details implying this fact in the biographies of such patriots as Ivan Franko and Mykhailo Dragomanov. When the Bolsheviks started as the big political force, they quickly became the enemy of any sort of Ukrainian nationalism and condemned it as "bourgeois." As the "Reds" were established in power in the region, they started all sorts of criminal persecutions against the Ukrainian national movement. Later with the rise of fascism, Soviet propaganda started to depict the UPR as a proto-fascist regime and Ukrainian nationalists as "classical" fascists.

Socialist ideas in general, however, were quite popular among Ukrainian nationalists. Ivan Franko was an active participant in the socialist movement and a founder of the socialist-oriented political party in Galicia. Socialism was especially strong among the UPR elite, and this was one of the major reasons they did not perceive Bolsheviks as enemies until it was too late.

Socialists and pro-socialist parties were extremely popular in Ukraine among the simple citizens too. Lenin and the Bolsheviks promised Ukrainian farmers the fulfillment of their greatest dream — land ownership. The similar ideas about freedom and the right for economic prosperity were popular among the urban proletariat. These were some of the key reasons for people to fight against pro-UPR military forces in some of the key events of the period.

People in the Russian Empire were tired of war, corruption, and the nobles who still dominated in the sphere of both economics and politics. Despite the Reform of 1861, farmers were still dependent on the people of noble descent, and the workers at factories engaged in heavy labor practically without any social rights and on the verge of poverty. Bolshevik propaganda was extremely efficient because it addressed the actual problems of the population not only in metropoles, but also in the provinces, including the territory of Ukraine.

The UPR officials were being torn apart between the masses who were inclined to support "leftists," old elites who were interested in supporting the status quo, and young nationalist forces that wanted to support the old economic system but with a new "answer" to the "national question." In this way, there was a general lack of unity among the UPR government in an ideological sense. Whatever decisions were made, there was always a large group of people who became dissatisfied with these politics.

To study the history of the UPR period is impossible without taking the First World War into consideration. As Russian historian Struve said, everything that unfolds in the world's history after the Great War will be the logical continuation of this event in different forms. That is to a certain extent debatable, but for the UPR period, the connection between the two events is absolutely evident.

The First World War was a child of its time. Historians and economists usually connect this great event to the redistribution of the spheres of influence between old masters of the world and new nations. These spheres include both markets to sell product and colonies in Africa and Asia that were the sources of great wealth and political influence.

In this sense, the fate of Ukrainian lands during and shortly after the conflict is symptomatic. Was Ukraine a colony? You definitely cannot call this country a colony in the classical sense. Ukrainian lands, however, served as the source of resources and military manpower for both sides of the conflict. Great states violated the rights and cultural legacy of the local population by making it take part in its military actions without giving the identity of the Ukrainians the slightest consideration.

There is definitely a lot of material for colonial and postcolonial studies here. There is also a question about whether Ukraine was a neocolony for Soviet Moscow after 1921 because the situation was similar to that with the Bolsheviks—they used Ukraine as a source of resources and manpower and suppressed the national identity on an even bigger scale than their predecessors. Nevertheless, it is hard to state something definite without engaging in a discussion about the definition of particular terms.

On June 28, 1914, Archduke Franz Ferdinand, a royal from Austria-Hungary, was assassinated in Sarajevo by Serbian nationalists. At that time, the political situation in the Balkans was extremely complex. There were several groups of people who were interested in destabilizing the region, including the secret services of some of the neighboring countries and independent terrorist organizations.

What is more, most of the Balkan region's population was ethnically Slavic, so this was a sphere of interest for the Russian Empire. Russia supported Serbia in its political struggles, and the events that unfolded after the famous assassination drove the country into the Great War despite its numerous economic and internal political problems.

At that time, the Russian Empire was still recovering from a devastating war with Japan (1904–05) and the resulting political instability. The campaign showed that Russian armed forces, although big in numbers, failed to keep pace with the progress of military tactics and strategy, resulting in the defeat of the empire by the island country.

The resulting political impact triggered instability in the Russian Empire. While there were a few positive reforms, they all were ended later by the tsar, who regained all the lost power and influence but sowed even more dissatisfaction in society in return. Other countries that witnessed the defeats of the Russian Army in the campaign made changes to their international politics (including ambitions concerning some of the Russian territories).

The diplomatic game around the beginning of the Great War and the events that involved Russia in the war are an interesting topic for a separate research project. As for Ukraine and its history, it is important to emphasize the tragedy of that event for the population—Ukrainians as citizens of the two different sides of the conflict often had to face their own in the battle. Nevertheless, the experience some participants gained during these conflicts was very important for the later development of the UPR army as well as other military forces.

On July 28, 1914, Austria-Hungary declared war on Serbia and triggered the chain of events that lead to the Great War. Two big opposing blocks of countries formed—the Central Powers and the Allied Forces (Entente). The Central Powers included Austria-Hungary, Germany, the Ottoman Empire, and Bulgaria. The Entente included France, the British Empire, Italy (from 1915), and some other countries. Russia was a part of the Entente until the crisis of 1917, which also concerns the event establishing the Ukrainian People's Republic.

The Central Powers fought on two main fronts in Europe (not including colonial campaigns) — the Western Front and the Eastern Front. The events and factors that concern the topic of this book are mostly connected to the Eastern Front. Some of the major battles of the Great War happened in the territory of Ukraine, and the campaign, in general, had global consequences for the politics of the region. The short story of the Western Front and the general timeline of the War, however, should be outlined too.

For a few years, the Western Front did not move far although hard battles were waged with extreme casualties from both sides of the conflict. Some of the bloodiest of these battles include those of the Somme, the Marne, Verdun, and Passchendaele. On April 6, 1917, the United States joined the conflict on the Entente's side.

Eventually, the Central Powers, despite massive military power and resources, lost. German nationalists, especially in the times of Hitler, blamed the internal conflict and political activity of the leftists and socialists inside the country rather than the objective situation on the frontline. On November 11, 1918, the armistice was signed between Germany and the Allied Forces that ended one of the most devastating conflicts in the history of humanity.

Now we continue with a more detailed analysis of the events on the Eastern Front. On August 17, 1914, the Russian Empire declared war on Austria-Hungary and immediately invaded East Prussia. From August 29 to 31, 1914, the Battle of Tannenberg happened and was a complete defeat for Russia. It was followed by a totally unsuccessful offensive in the territory of Galicia in 1915. The Russian Empire had to retreat deeper into its own territory.

What were the reasons for such painful military defeats of the once-great Empire? The Russo-Japanese War was a bitter lesson, but that lesson was eventually in vain. No serious reforms of the Russian Army were made, and apart from tactical and strategic flaws, the supply lines were very poor, resulting in a lack of ammunition and artillery shells. Russian General Headquarters also lacked talented generals with free initiative.

The circumstances for the simple Russian soldiers were also quite bad. Because of the undersupply and command problems, the Russian Army suffered heavy losses. Austria-Hungary conducted its propaganda campaigns. Communists agitated on the frontline, and this agitation was quite successful given the circumstances. This, and the general fatigue from the battles and war, were reasons for them to revolt later and join the pro-Bolshevik forces.

These are all the preceding factors and circumstances for the later Revolution one of its consequences of which was the rise of the Ukrainian People's Republic. In 1916, the Russian Empire made one of its last successful military operations — the Brusilov Offensive. Despite the tactical success, the Offensive was not developed strategically. In February of 1917, the Revolution started, and the tsar was overthrown by Kerensky.

The February Revolution was a reason for major political unrest in all of the regions of the Russian Empire, including the territory of today's Ukraine. Representatives of the national opposition thought it was a great chance to gain political autonomy in the newly founded liberal regime.

One of the key organizations of Ukrainian intellectuals was SUP (the Society of Ukrainian Progressives [Товариство українських поступовців]). As the name hints, this organization wanted to achieve national goals in the course of step-by-step evolution rather than radical changes. The first step of that evolution should have been a limited political autonomy.

SUP was probably one of the most influential national political organizations, but it had rivals in both more radical nationalists and socialists. SUP initiated the creation of the ruling organs of the UPR, but, in fact, after their creation, SUP became a political minority in the state because of the influence of those rivals. SUP was eventually re-organized into a socialist-federalist political party.

As was the case in the pre-Revolution period, the opposition included some radical thinkers who dreamed of proclaiming complete political independence, but their influence was small until the next political events when, in March 1917, Ukrainian national opposition created the Ukrainian Central Council. Mykhailo Hrushevsky, a famous historian, was later elected as the Head of the Council. This organ became a parliament of the young Ukrainian state with representatives from different classes of society.

The process of consultations with Kerensky began. At least during the first stages of the process, both sides of the controversy strived to avoid military and economic confrontation. Central authorities, however, did not really want to give newly formed Ukraine much political autonomy. As the famous quotation says, "Russian liberalism ends where the Ukrainian question begins." This controversy was the reason for a long diplomatic game that eventually was in vain: the new Bolshevik authorities who soon gained power saw the global picture in a completely different way. Their methods of supporting their ideology were also much more "direct" and connected to the immediate military actions.

Kerensky eventually refused the Ukrainian side on the question of political autonomy. UPR officials had to take action. Central authorities were still unable to foster discipline among their troops or use the massive military forces. And there was still a chance that, in this unstable situation, courageous political actions would bring practical results. The Ukrainian Central Council declared its First Universal on June 23 (OS June 10), 1917, a document that proclaimed the political autonomy of Ukraine within the borders of the Russian state.

The ruling organ of the UPR was created—a General Secretary, which was headed by a famous public figure, Volodymyr Vynnychenko. Vynnychenko was quite an interesting character in Ukrainian politics of that time. He was an extremely influential figure among UPR officials as well as national intelligence in general, and he had socialist political views that he did not hide from the public. His views were the reason for several unexpected important turns in the UPR's politics. In the last phase of the existence of the UPR, Vynnychenko was de facto head of the state.

Nevertheless, Kerensky was still in power, and consultations between his government and the UPR continued. There was a danger of military escalation, and UPR officials had to find a compromise. These events led to the proclamation of the Second Universal. This new document canceled the political autonomy of the Ukrainian People's Republic and stated that the question of independence should be posed after the all-state Constituent Assembly. Part of society perceived this Universal as a betrayal.

Eventually, it became the reason for a riot among the military. On July 17 (OS July 4), 1917, a second Ukrainian regiment named after Pavlo Polubotok started a rebellion. It was, however, quickly suppressed by the regular Russian army loyal to the Central Authorities. The UPR supported this decision as well.

That was not the last military clash in Kyiv. Pro-Soviet historians usually claim that the UPR was never a state because of such a huge number of different political crises and military riots. Besides such main operations as the Bolshevik sieges of the city, there were several different clashes between different political factions that were often supported by military forces. As a result, these historians claim that the UPR was rather an ideological and political project than a real state.

In August 1917, the Central Authorities acknowledged the UPR governmental body as its representative on the territory of Ukraine. The UPR continued on its political course toward gaining political autonomy. Meanwhile, another hidden revolutionary force—Bolsheviks—was growing in popularity both in the central regions of the Empire and the territory of Ukraine.

On November 7 (OS October 25), 1917, a second Revolution happened in Petrograd. The radical communist party came to power instead of Kerensky. The leader of the Bolsheviks was Vladimir Lenin. On the next day, the Bolshevik rebellion happened in Kyiv. This time, however, the UPR and its supporting military forces were stronger than the rebels. The Ukrainian People's Republic was still in control of the city.

Bolsheviks were even more strict on the question of Ukrainian autonomy than Kerensky. Lenin did not see another option than Ukraine as a part of a new Soviet state. This eventually brought about a big, open conflict between two states that was the main reason for the UPR's release of the Third Universal. The

Third Universal again proclaimed the political autonomy of the Ukrainian People's Republic as part of the Russian State.

The Third Universal added some new land to the body of the UPR and announced that Ukraine and Ukrainian forces were withdrawing from participation in the First World War. Could this be assessed morally as well? This question is not that popular among the pro-Soviet and pro-Russian debaters because Bolsheviks actually also had diplomatic contacts regarding ending participation in that conflict. This question is more interesting for a professional historian.

If we continue the line of the moral condemnation of Mazepa-like political actions, then we should condemn that decision as well. It is not as ambiguous as the Nazi collaboration in the Second World War, but the Kaiser's Germany was the aggressive, imperialistic state that led a war of conquest and had values opposed to those of the Russian Empire. But, then again, we should also blame the Bolsheviks for this "sin."

Apart from the myths about the inception of Ukrainians as a nation, there are also political myths about the Bolsheviks' role in geopolitics and especially the war with Germany. It is often speculated that the Bolsheviks made a great deal to help the Central Powers while taking pressure off their soldiers on the Eastern Front. In this view, Vladimir Lenin was financed by the German authorities. and the whole October Revolution was provoked to weaken or overthrow the tsarist government.

Of course, this is more myth than proven historical facts. Nevertheless, understanding the mythology surrounding these events is vital to objective analysis. This mythology influences not only the historical perception of the mentioned events, but also contemporary ideology and even contemporary politics.

The Bolsheviks possessed more than military power in the area of Ukraine. They were also extremely popular among the population in a political sense. Perhaps the main argument for them among the villagers was the communist approach to landowner policy. The UPR is often blamed for its support of the big landowners and the absence of any profound reforms in this sector. Pro-Soviet historians even claim this is firm evidence that the whole UPR project was about saving the status quo for agrarian oligarchs and building a system where they were in power instead of the aristocrats.

It was indeed true that, at a certain point, the UPR proclaimed land to be in the state's ownership, in one program with the socialist view on things. There were, however, numerous problems in the implementation of that legal initiative. The progress was later revoked by different laws during the Skoropadsky era.

One example of a rich and educated Ukrainian of progressive views was Yevhen Chykalenko. He is an interesting figure in Ukrainian history known mostly by professional historians. Chykalenko was a rich farmer and landowner who financed many projects connected to the Ukrainian national movement, including the printing of the first Ukrainian political newspaper *Rada* [*Рада*]. Prior to the Skoropadsky era, Chykalenko was considered as one of the candidates for the role of Hetman.

Chykalenko was a great sympathizer of the Ukrainian movement who gave much of his financial resources to supporting it. He was an influential figure in the movement, but he declined the offer to be the head of the state. Pro-Soviet historians and journalists would say he was one of those oligarchs for whom the "project of the UPR" was created. From their point of view, his cultural activity was actually ideological, political, and the means to more wealth and influence in society.

However questionable these speculations are, failing to meet the demands of the public was one of the main reasons for the failure of the Ukrainian People's Republic. Meanwhile, the Bolsheviks were gaining more and more political power among UPR citizens. There were communist representatives in every committee, and they created numerous political organizations, some of which were paramilitary. This played an important role in the next events.

The Third Universal provoked the first war between the Ukrainian People's Republic and Soviet Russia. At the end of November 1917, another communist rebellion happened in Kyiv, but it was quickly suppressed by loyal military forces. As a result,

Soviet officials posed a demand to the UPR: give away political autonomy. Together with that demand was political activity in the committees by the Bolsheviks, who tried to overthrow or weaken UPR influence by means of democratic mechanisms.

Eventually, however, the committees mostly supported the UPR and its course of actions, and the demand was declined. As a response, on December 22 (OS December 9), 1917, the Red Guard occupied Kharkiv and created an alternative governmental body for Ukraine with a capital in this city. On January 7, 1918 (OS December 25, 1917), 30,000 Bolshevik army troops started the offensive on the city of Kyiv.

On February 9 (OS January 27), 1918, the Ukrainian People's Republic proclaimed its Fourth (and last) Universal. This document stated the complete independence of Ukraine as a state. It also proclaimed a course of political and military struggle with Soviet Russia. Nevertheless, it was not very effective; so much time was already lost.

After the occupation of Kharkiv, the UPR stated that it wanted to take part in international relations and diplomacy separately from Soviet Russia. A separate Ukrainian delegation joined the Brest-Litovsk Peace Treaty consultations. Soviet delegates were utterly unsatisfied with such a turn of events. There are some speculations that this detail, in particular, worsened the diplomatic games of the Soviets drastically. This is, however, impossible to prove as a fact.

In January 1918, the Bolshevik army sieged Kyiv and eventually captured it. It was precisely during this time that the discussed Kruty Battle happened. It was mostly analyzed in the previous chapter, but it is useful to revisit the general context.

A few hundred of the young Ukrainians marched to the railway station near Kyiv hoping to defeat Bolsheviks. Many of them died in the battle. Whether it was useful (bought some time for the UPR Command) or useless is speculation. It is, however, evident that this event is sacred to Ukrainian national culture.

Government officials of the UPR had to leave the city. The Ukrainians retreated to the city of Zhytomyr. The Bolsheviks started a campaign of terror against the citizens of the city and killed as many as 5000 civilians whom they suspected to be "enemies of the Revolution." They would have captured the remaining territory, but the UPR found its salvation in the help of former opponents—the Austro-Hungarian and German armies.

The Ukrainian People's Republic asked the Germans to help, and they sent their troops to capture the remaining territory of Ukraine. They defeated the Bolsheviks and freed Kyiv together with some other regions of Ukraine, including the Crimean peninsula.

The main interest for the Central Powers was not political control over Ukrainian territories but the agrarian resources the country possessed. The Germans obligated the UPR with huge food reparations to help the Central Powers, who were in exhausted economic shape, prolonging the fight on the Western Front.

The Ukrainian People's Republic government returned to the capital. The Germans, however, were not satisfied with their new ally. The UPR could not provide the agrarian reparation in full volume because of the general lack of political and social stability, the lack of discipline among the local representative organs, and strong opposition toward that policy among simple Ukrainian farmers.

Eventually, it led to a coup d'état supported by the Central Powers. Now, it was an authoritarian regime headed by proclaimed Hetman Pavlo Skoropadsky. The Ukrainian Central Committee was dissolved, and the country was called the Ukrainian State instead of the Ukrainian People's Republic.

Skoropadsky was a former Russian general and a descendant of one of the last hetmans of Ukraine from the classic Cossack era. He was an authoritarian leader who strived to support the social status quo, including the role of aristocracy and the pressing question of land ownership. In fact, his politics were pure conservatism. This led to the deep dissatisfaction of the lower class of the population and an even bigger growth of support for socialist and communist ideology in Ukrainian society.

The Germans were eventually defeated on the Western Front, mostly due to social instability and economic problems.

They had to withdraw their forces from Ukraine, and Skoropadsky was left without serious military support. It was only a matter of time before he was to be overthrown. In November and December 1918, the Anti-Hetman Uprising happened and was led by the previously mentioned Volodymyr Vynnychenko and Simon Petlura.

The uprising was successful. Skoropadsky had to leave the country. It was proclaimed that the Ukrainian People's Republic had been reestablished, but now the central government body of the state was the so-called Directory headed by Volodymyr Vynnychenko. The Directory defined the new state's socialist politics.

A new parliament-like organ was formed—the Working Congress instead of the Ukrainian Central Committee—but all the key decisions were taken by the Directory. The army and military started to play a bigger role in the life of the state, which defined the serious influence in society gained by Simon Petlura.

Simon Petlura is an interesting character. He began as a military-affiliated official, and in 1919, he became the new Head of the Directory instead of Vynnychenko. Ukrainian nationalist-oriented intellectuals consider him a hero, whereas pro-Soviet debaters blame him for mass persecutions of the Jewish population and militaristic, even ultranational, politics. For Russians, Petlura is an awful villain in along the same vein as Mazepa and Bandera. He was assassinated later by a person of Jewish origin while living in exile in Paris. The assassin claimed it was an act of revenge for the persecutions of Jews through which his relatives suffered.

Meanwhile, after German support ceased, the Bolsheviks decided to make their move. The second war with Soviet Russia started. UPR military forces were not ready this time either. The only realistic hope for the young state to defend itself lay in the field of diplomacy.

A UPR delegation took part in the Paris Peace Conference of 1919. This "diplomatic battle," however, was eventually lost as well. Such big players as Great Britain and France were against weakening Russia as a state, and their main bet was supporting Poland. The fact that the UPR military forces were disorganized and weak as well as the enormous popularity of the socialist ideas among the state's officials also played their role.

In November 1918, the new state on the territory of Ukraine that had been under the rule of Austria-Hungary was proclaimed—The Western Ukrainian Republic. The new state had an open military conflict with neighboring Poland. Czechoslovakia and The Kingdom of Romania also pretended to take some regions of the newly formed state. On January 22, 1919, the Western Ukrainian Republic and the Ukrainian People's Republic proclaimed an Act of Unification creating the single unified country with some autonomy for the WUR.

All these circumstances led to a situation whereby the UPR had to fight Bolsheviks, Poland, Romania, and different insurgent gangs simultaneously. The phenomenon is known as the Ukrainian "Death Triangle". In the beginning of 1919, there was only a small piece of territory near Kamenetz Podolsk under the UPR control. In February 1919, Bolsheviks recaptured Kyiv. The UPR army managed to recapture the city in September 1919.

Meanwhile, the remnants of the Russian Imperial Army—the so-called White Movement headed by former Russian military leader Anton Denikin—started an offensive from the Crimean peninsula to the north, eventually besieging Kyiv again. There was an idea among some of UPR leaders to make a temporary alliance with the White Movement to defeat the Bolsheviks, but that faction was too chauvinist toward any measure of Ukrainian independence.

Eventually, the Whites defeated Petlura's forces and captured Kyiv. They then began their offensive toward Moscow but were defeated by the Bolsheviks in their turn. That event marked the final phase of the White Movement. Soon it was completely wiped out by Reds. In the end of 1919, most of the territory of Transnistrian Ukraine was under complete control of the Red Army. The Bolsheviks established a new Ukrainian Soviet Socialist Republic there.

Things turned out extremely bad for the Ukrainian People's Republic. Desperate measures were taken: the UPR decided to make contact with its former enemy, Poland. A diplomatic mission was sent to Warsaw to negotiate peace and a possible military alliance against the Bolsheviks. Some of the territories of the western regions of Ukraine were given away, sacrificed in the name of prolonging the existence of the state. Of course, this was viewed as a betrayal by the Ukrainian population of the western regions. The Act of Unification was denounced.

At that time, the Directory was not, in fact, extant. Petlura was in charge of the remnants of the official UPR organs and military forces. In the end of 1919 and until May 1920, the Ukrainian Army made the so-called First Winter Campaign, providing mostly partisan actions behind the lines of the Bolsheviks and the Whites.

On April 25, 1920, the UPR made the military alliance with Poland official and started the offensive against the Red Army. They managed to recapture Kyiv once again but eventually were defeated by the Bolsheviks. The Polish-Ukrainian Army had to retreat to the territory of Poland. The Ukrainian People's Republic was no more.

There was some activity from the UPR government in exile as well as the Second Winter Campaign, but all in all, the period of the Ukrainian People's Republic met its tragic end. The Second Winter Campaign was much less successful than the First, and it ended in the mass killing of Ukrainian soldiers by the Red Army and Cheka near the village of Bazar. In the history of Ukraine, this latest episode is considered a tragic event in the same vein as the Battle of Kruty.

What can be said about the general context of Ukraine in 2013–22? Perhaps the most important and global preceding event is the collapse of the Soviet Union and Ukraine gaining its independence after almost 70 years as a province of the Empire.

Ukraine shares many common problems with other former Soviet republics that gained independence at about the same time. These problems are poverty, corruption, and sociopolitical instability. People with a pro-Soviet position tend to claim that these are not the problems of the period of political transition but rather the first attribute of being incorporated into the capitalistic world with the status of a third-rate colony.

Throughout the years, the elite of Ukraine was formed: a small percent of super-rich people own more than 90 percent of the nation's resources—from natural resources to the service sector. These people are not public figures, and the changes in the hierarchy since 1991 are negligible.

Of course, this situation brings political instability as a consequence. There were several serious political conflicts in the history of independent Ukraine that concerned the distribution of resources and social justice more than just as a "national question." You can draw analogies with a popular socialist concept that a "national question" is actually artificially invented by the imperialists to draw attention away from the ever-present, real question of social justice and class struggle.

You can easily compare this situation to that of the Austro-Hungarian part of Ukraine. Galychyna was an underdeveloped rural region going through the changes of the beginning of capitalism, whereas other regions of the country were already in a "developed" phase.

The conflict between the old elites and the newly formed big capital was inevitable. It brought all sorts of social and political tensions. This process also concerned Ukrainians, who were the least socially protected group in the region. The clashes and tragedies of this conflict are described in the novels of Ivan Franko, for example.

The only alternative to the revolution in this situation is making reforms and hoping that the new generation of Ukrainians will create a more just society step-by-step. Meanwhile, pro-Russian debaters claim that this situation is not a sign of internal problems but rather the consequence of Ukraine being a neo-colony such that the "way of reforms" is utopic and futile.

The collapse of the Soviet Union is again often assessed from the moral viewpoint. It is rarely claimed that its economy was ineffective, and it is emphasized that a socialist economic system was justified in general, especially when the distribution of resources is concerned. The internationalism and the linguistic unity of the population of the country were considered virtues.

This again can be compared to the situation in the beginning of Bolshevik reign over the territory of Ukraine. There was a lot of enthusiasm in society toward the new social order and production, including the cultural sector. Many people who took part in the previous conflict on the side of the Red Army had ambitions to develop the culture, including the authentic national culture of Ukraine.

For complex reasons, in the first phase of this process, the Bolsheviks were quite liberal toward developing the language and national culture. It ended, however, in mass persecutions for those engaged in this activity.

In this way, the first years after the collapse of the USSR in Ukraine were marked both with astonishing political achievements for the newly formed, independent Ukraine and the many problems connected to poverty and corruption (e.g., ineffective production, an extremely high unemployment rate, the rise of organized crime, and the degradation of cultural institutions).

Apart from the socioeconomic problems, there were serious cultural issues arising in the society. The core problem was the question of Ukrainian and Russian language usage. In the Soviet Union, the usage of the Russian language in official documentation and the public sphere was strongly supported. The Ukrainian language was not officially prohibited, but it was banished from the public sphere. Besides that, the general Ukrainian culture, including the books in this language and the scientific research on the history of Ukraine as a separate state, was considered marginal.

Ukrainian culture was mostly unsupported in the public sector, and people engaged in developing it were considered suspicious. After the collapse of the Soviet Union, new ways to develop the culture and language emerged, but the social environment changed drastically. Production, including the cultural sector, had to follow the laws of the market economy.

Now, the factor of popularity played a great role in the success of the cultural project. Most of the market is dominated by Russian language products because most of the population of the country, especially in the eastern and southern regions, speaks this language instead of Ukrainian. It is extremely hard for Ukrainian language products to find a niche.

The role of language with a new context continued to play an important role in politics. It would be one of the triggering mechanisms for the processes and radical changes of 2013.

The first president of independent Ukraine, Leonid Kravchuk, was the representative of the Party elite. He mostly supported the status quo in society and is blamed both by nationalists and communists not only for lack of action in the sphere of social reforms, but also for systemic corruption.

Corruption and the resulting poverty are problems of independent Ukraine that never were dealt with in any of the stages of the state's existence. Organized crime ceased to be such a powerful factor in the country's politics after the 1990s, but corrupt politicians as well as completely uncontrolled regional elites remain actual problems today.

Kravchuk lost the next elections to Leonid Kuchma, another representative of the Soviet elite. Kuchma tried to strike a balance in international relations between the West and the Russian Federation. His rule, however, was marked with several big scandals.

Probably the biggest scandal was connected to the murder of the journalist Georgy Gongadze in 2000. Political opponents of the President published records of several discussions among Kuchma and his close circles about Gongadze's anti-corruption investigations that implied Leonid Kuchma might have ordered the killing of the journalist. This scandal triggered a series of political demonstrations for a "Ukraine without Kuchma" with bloody clashes between the protesters and riot police. At that time, however, Kuchma managed to mitigate the crisis and stay in power.

The next big crisis started in 2004 with the new presidential election. Kuchma was about to hand over power to his chosen successor, Viktor Yanukovich, who was a pro-Russian candidate with a crime-affiliated past (he even served time in prison). His opponent was Viktor Yushchenko, a candidate with pro-Western values.

Kuchma gave major administrative support to Yanukovich, from media support to support of government representatives on all levels. The election was extremely tense. It reached its peak when, after the second tour of the campaign, Yanukovich was proclaimed President.

The supporters of Yushchenko started the global protest later known as the Orange Revolution. After a few months of crisis, the government called another election, which was won by Yushchenko this time. The supporters of Yanukovich were deeply dissatisfied.

The Orange Revolution was symptomatic of the situation in Ukrainian society. It was a first major clash of the big groups inside it that positioned the question of language, culture, and international relations at the center of the events.

Yushchenko was associated with the usage of the Ukrainian language, a close connection to the European Union and the USA, as well as movement toward the West in general. For his part, Yanukovich was a representative with close association to the Soviet past, connections to Russia, and traditional conservative values and social institutions. These facts would play an even bigger role in the future.

Yushchenko was a triumphant winner of an extremely tense election campaign. He had huge support on the international level as well as from most of the population of Ukraine. He proved, however, to be incompetent and a weak leader. His former allies started to gain more influence, which eventually brought a conflict and the crisis that resulted in Yanukovich and his supporters returning to power. In 2010, Viktor Yanukovich won the election and became the President of Ukraine.

His presidency was marked with many scandals connected to corruption as well as anti-Ukrainian national politics. An important element of these politics was ceasing international relations with the West and building new close connections to Russia. Yanukovich was also using his political resources to gain extreme wealth for himself and his close circle.

This brought about a very complex political and social situation at the end of 2013. People were extremely dissatisfied. It only needed a spark for the fire to ignite, and the Association Agreement with the European Union became that spark.

The Association Agreement with the European Union was a phase of integrative and cooperative politics between Ukraine and Europe that was designed in the 1990s. This document should have integrated the Ukrainian economic and political system deeper into that of the EU in a major step for the hypothetical future admission to the EU. Signing this document, however, was not in Yanukovich's political program because it would harm relations with Russia.

It is debatable whether there are economic minuses to that program. The topic is very hot as it concerns one of the central myths of the Ukrainian nation (European or Asian identity). Nevertheless, it is evident that, for Yanukovich, relations with Russia and staying in power were more important than anything else.

In November 2013, the Ukrainian government canceled the previously negotiated preparation process for the signing of the Agreement. It had a major impact on the social situation in Ukraine. A group of young people and students started a protest in the center of Kyiv (Maidan). They established a tent camp.

On November 30, 2013, the students were beaten by riot police, which started the series of bloody and tragic events later named the Revolution of Dignity or Maidan Revolution. The protests came to involve large masses of the population.

By different estimations, on some days after November 30, there were from 500,000 to 1 million protesters at Maidan. Opposition leaders tried to "ride the wave" and established the National Resistance Headquarters. It is doubtful, however, that the process of protest was controlled even to some extent by this or other ruling structures.

Pro-Russian sources claim that, as in the case of the Orange Revolution, this protest was inspired, financed, and controlled by Western agents of influence associated mostly with the CIA and NATO. In their words, the Revolution of Dignity was the advancement of the theory of "colored revolutions" and was the part of the game for influence in Eastern Europe between Russia and the West. The similar events in Serbia and Georgia are also mentioned to emphasize that the struggle is more about control of the global region than about Ukraine or its culture. The pro-Ukrainian position condemns such claims as propaganda.

A full-scale political crisis had begun. Protesters tried to storm the President's Office, and they captured some of the administrative buildings in the central area of the city. Every day, there were more and more clashes with the police force.

There were already victims of these clashes on both sides, protesters and riot police. A Ukrainian riot police task force group known as "Berkut" (Eagle) came to play a serious role in the events that unfolded. Protesters usually claim that this task force was inappropriately cruel and already had left a wake of many savage beatings in the first phase of the protest. Pro-Russian debaters claim that there were victims among police and conscripts already and that the task force's actions were meant to stop the escalation. Berkut's former members are considered heroes by the pro-Russian debaters and often continued military service among Russian or separatist forces.

On January 16, 2014, Ukrainian Parliament introduced a group of new laws that severely narrowed the freedom and rights of citizens. The laws were aimed at stopping the protest but instead escalated them even more. Clashes continued. On January 22, a tragic event occurred—the first officially confirmed killed protesters. The consultations and negotiations between the opposition and the government were ongoing. It seemed, however, that the opposition had no real control over the process of the Revolution nor did the government.

The tent camp at Maidan was stormed many times by police forces. Protesters built barricades and used stones and even Molotov cocktails to protect the tent camp. The conflict reached its peak in February 2014, when more than one hundred protesters were killed by police snipers. Government was paralyzed. Yanukovich had to flee the country.

Parliament brought back the pre-2004 variant of the constitution and called a presidential election. Petro Poroshenko became the new President of Ukraine. Poroshenko was a pro-European politician and a wealthy businessman, even an oligarch. Poroshenko was an experienced political administrator and diplomat. His critics, however, usually mention corruption during his presidency and his use of political tools for personal gain and PR.

The reaction of the Russian Federation to the events of the Revolution of Dignity was utterly negative. Russian officials commented on the events as the illegal overthrow of the officially elected President and government. Maidan's activists were blamed as provocateurs, ultranationalists, and fascists. It was Russian President Vladimir Putin who helped Yanukovich to flee the country and sanctioned the next tragic military events.

In February 2014, the Russian annexation of the Crimean peninsula began. Crimea was always problematic for the pro-national forces of Ukraine; most of the population spoke the Russian language and supported pro-Russian forces. Nevertheless, the ethnic minority of Crimean Tatars were usually anti-Russian due to historical and social reasons and mostly sided with Ukraine in the conflict with the Russian Federation.

During the times of an independent Ukraine, the Crimean peninsula was an autonomous federative node with its own parliament, and the city of Sevastopol, which was the home of a Russian Federation military navy base, had special status. In the Revolution of Dignity, the ruling organs of the peninsula as well as most of the politically active groups sided with Yanukovich.

In the end of February 2014, unidentified military groups started to appear in Crimea, establishing checkpoints and occupying such key locations as administrative buildings and military bases. This unknown military force was later closely associated with the Russian military. Judging from the later political recognition of the participants of these events in Russian society, it is officially confirmed that they were part of the sanctioned military operation. The force was composed of some special forces elite operatives as well as volunteers and members of different patriotic paramilitary organizations.

Most of the military bases held by the Ukrainian Army were blockaded, and after several days of the continuing pressure, gave up. They often left behind their military equipment for the Russians to use in the future. Unfortunately, there were episodes with fatal casualties among Ukrainian soldiers.

In mid-March 2014, a referendum concerning Crimea joining the Russian Federation was held. According to the official results, most of the population voted for it. The political part of the annexation of Crimea by Russian forces was complete.

This act of annexation is a very debatable topic in terms of international relations and international law. Russians claim they were completely justified in this to protect the Russian-speaking population of Crimea who definitely had pro-Russian political views. In this vein, the Ukrainian Revolution of Dignity was an illegal revolt inspired by the intelligence services of Western countries that had brought radical nationalists to power.

Ukrainians claim that annexation is an utter violation of international laws, including some of the specific agreements between Russia and Ukraine. The Budapest Memorandum on Security Assurances in connection with Ukraine's accession to the Treaty on the Non-Proliferation of Nuclear Weapons is often mentioned in this context. It was an agreement whereby Ukraine liquidated its nuclear weapons and production facilities in exchange for guarantees of security.

The agreement was, in fact, violated as no countries that signed that agreement sent their troops to assist Ukraine during the annexation and the war in the Donbass region. The same thing happened with the military intervention of the Russian Federation in the beginning of 2022 (although lethal weapons and military equipment are now sent to the country).

Pro-Russian debaters usually state that the overthrow of Yanukovich broke the status quo, including this and similar international documents. They again insist that protecting the Russian-speaking population is a moral obligation of the Russian government.

That is actually a very interesting detail for contemporary philosophy of law. Ukrainians base their claims on specific legal documents and agreements, whereas Russia claims the moral side of things. This is the same as in the cases of the World Wars and Hetman Mazepa. Nevertheless, if we admit that international documents have moral obligations as well, the picture becomes even more complicated.

The international diplomatic community condemned the annexation as a severe violation of international laws, probably the most severe since the Second World War. In March 2014, the United Nations General Assembly declared the annexation invalid. The majority of the participant states supported the declaration. Some specialists claim that the act of illegal annexation "cancels" all the diplomatic efforts at building international security in Europe for the last 70 years.

In the international community, Russia is supported by some countries in South America, to which it is connected by tight economic connections, as well as countries of Global South. The biggest diplomatic support Russia gets, however, is from China. Chinese diplomats state a neutral position toward the conflict in Ukraine but exert a lot of effort to protect Russia from international pressure.

In this respect, the conflict in Ukraine is just a little piece of a bigger conflict between China and the United States of America for political and economic dominance in the world. The stakes in this game are very high. Both parties are very careful because open conflict automatically leads to the usage of nuclear weapons and confirmation of the mutually-assured-destruction doctrine.

Ukraine and Russia are viewed as proxies that create a field where the indirect diplomatic and intelligence efforts of both parties shape and reshape the balance of power in the region and consequently the world. The situation is similar to the first years of the Cold War when any local regional conflict automatically became a chess match between Stalin and the West.

Today's world is more complicated economically and technologically, and these "chess moves" become more subtle and complex, involving more areas of everyday life, like culture and computer technologies. Anyone who wants to resolve the conflict in Ukraine should take the global picture into consideration.

The conflict in the Donbass region of Ukraine developed in parallel with the annexation. Donbass was another "problematic" region for pro-Ukrainian forces. Donetsk and Luhansk Oblast are inhabited mostly by a Russian-speaking population with a strong sentiment toward the Soviet past. It also was the home region of

Viktor Yanukovich and most of his political associates. Most of his electoral support was from this region and Crimea.

Yanukovich and his supporters spread propaganda that mostly emphasized the economic role of the region and the problem of Russian language usage. The inhabitants of the western regions of Ukraine were introduced as an alien, pro-Western culture that strives to deny the social status of the eastern population, cut any cultural ties with Russia as well as their Soviet past, and use Ukraine as a neo-colony and market for their products.

In early spring, the region was infiltrated by special forces groups similar to the situation in Crimea. They also made alliances with local paramilitary organizations and pro-Russian political activists. One of those groups was led by Ihor Girkin (who uses the pseudonym "Strelkov"), a former FSS (Russian Federal Security Service) operative and a member of the historical reconstruction movement who would play a major media role for the separatists in future.

Separatists quickly captured two big cities, Donetsk and Luhansk, and began to move deeper into the territory of Ukraine. Pro-Russian forces used what later would be called "hybrid war." They only used spec ops forces in some situations, mostly concentrating on backing up paramilitary organizations and civil protesters. Media showed the political conflict inside Ukrainian society rather than the armed insurgency supported by the neighboring country.

The involvement of the Russian military and secret service as well as the scale of that involvement is the main topic for debates here. According to the Ukrainian point of view, the whole insurgency is orchestrated from Russia. The supplies and strike teams are all professional military and secret service operatives, and the vehicles, tanks, and artillery are of Russian origin. In this way, the whole insurgency is a hybrid war, a conflict that uses media and psychological operations to manipulate international opinion the same way that simple soldiers are fighting on the battlefield.

Russians, for their part, admit that there are a lot of volunteers from their country in Donbass, but they all moved there by their own moral choice. According to this position, Kyiv's government is, in fact, an ultranational military junta and their methods of countering the insurgency in the Donbass region are extremely cruel and fascist. The insurgency itself is genuine because it is composed mostly of locals with only limited support from international volunteers. And every separatist victory is a great deed by an unprofessional people's militia. As for the Ukrainian side, Russians claim that all the successful military operations are, in fact, guided by NATO and the CIA. This controversy is along the same vein as major historical controversies in Ukraine, including those from the UPR period, (e.g., the Battle of Kruty, Bazar, etc.).

Separatists were successful in the Donbass region. Their efforts, however, failed in Dnipropetrovsk, Zaporizhzhia, Kharkiv, etc. The grand plan was to spread insurgency across all of the east and south of the country, leaving only some central and western regions for the Ukrainian government to control. Nevertheless, in those regions, there were many more armed conflicts and much more violence. Pro-Russian debaters claim that this is when the Ukrainian government started to use loyal spec ops troops to counter the hybrid operations as well as the paramilitary organizations. Russians consider such organizations as "Azov" and "Right Sector" to be, in fact, neo-Nazi criminal gangs. Ukrainians claim a similar status for pro-Russian paramilitary.

The Ukrainian conflict in Donbass, just like any other regional military conflict, attracts mercenaries and radicals from all over the globe. It is indeed true that there are a lot of such radical people in the Ukrainian army, especially so in the beginning of the conflict. The same can be said about the separatists, however.

In May 2014, the Ukrainian government launched an official military operation to reclaim the lost territories and sovereignty. It was then called the ATO (Anti-Terrorist Operation) and later renamed JFO (Joint Forces Operation). At first, it was effective. The Ukrainian army and secret service operatives were bigger in numbers and more organized. The city of Slavyansk, the main base of separatists at that time, was sieged and captured. Girkin and his group had to retreat to Donetsk.

After that operation, the end of the war in favor of the Ukrainian government seemed inevitable. Ukrainian forces were closing on Donetsk and Luhansk and about to encircle them by recapturing posts at the eastern border of the country. Ihor Girkin made a famous public statement asking Russian President Vladimir Putin for help. The next events are viewed differently by Russia and Ukraine.

The Battle of Ilovaysk was mostly described in the previous chapter. It only needs some general political and diplomatic context. Ukrainian troops entered the city while the tide was on their side. Everyone was waiting for the final phase of the conflict. They were suddenly encircled by an overwhelming military force and suffered major casualties. During the negotiated retreat, they were shelled by Russian forces and suffered even more casualties.

Ukrainian officials and participants of the battle claim that the Russian army entered the region, thereby fully confirming its participation in the conflict. Separatists were mostly defeated at that time by the Ukrainian army. However, the Russian military was an overwhelming force against which Ukrainians did not stand a chance.

As for the separatist point of view, the Ukrainian group was indeed encircled with the help of Russians, but they were volunteers who could not remain neutral when their allies were being wiped out by the Ukrainians. The commanding center of the operation was still the "people's militia." Ukrainian military forces were pushed out of the region, and the conflict was moving to the "freezing" stage.

The first ceasefire agreement, known as the Minsk Protocol, was signed in September 2014. The central topic was a ceasefire, but, unfortunately, it did not last long. Both sides had a lot of losses and broke the agreement numerous times. There were also questions about the withdrawal of heavy weapons, POW exchange, and a monitoring mission by OSCE. The mode of political dialogue about searching for peace was proclaimed.

Another important event to mention is a tragedy that occurred in July 2014. Malaysian Airlines Flight MH17 was shot down while flying over separatist-controlled territory. All the passengers and crew on board were killed. Ukrainian officials blame the separatists' anti-air defense, whereas Russians place the blame on Ukrainian army provocation.

This tragedy had a major international impact. An international investigation committee was formed to scrutinize the details of the event and provide the trial for those involved. Ukrainian forces managed to capture a high-ranking "people's militia" anti-air officer at some point, claiming he was the commander who gave the order to shoot down the plane. He was exchanged, however, for Ukrainian captives later.

Apart from its direct political impact, this tragic event deeply characterizes the nature of the conflict between Russia and Ukraine. Everything has its media side, and everything is subject to informational and media manipulation. In this way, historians and political scientists as well as media public figures play a big role in the process of war. It seems that Jean Baudrillard's prognosis about the future mediatization of armed conflicts was really precise.

The conflict continued as a series of tactical battles until January 2015, when the Battle of Debaltseve began. Debaltseve was a transportation hub that connected Donetsk and Luhansk. It was controlled by Ukrainian armed forces, although both flanks were occupied by separatists. This hub was important for separatists both strategically and logistically.

The separatists launched an offensive and, after heavy fighting, captured the city, thereby drawing Ukrainian forces further to the west. It was the second major battle of the campaign, and as with the Battle of Ilovaysk, it was a defeat for the Ukrainian Army. Separatists encircled the Ukrainian army group, which was made to flee under heavy artillery shelling causing heavy casualties.

The question of casualties is very sensitive not only due to the tragic nature of the underlying event, but also due to politics and ideology. Russian security services and military intelligence, for obvious reasons, try to speculate on this question and draw a picture of enormous losses among simple soldiers caused by the incompetence and cowardice of their officers. This is very similar to the historical debates about UPR-era military clashes. At one point, the Ukrainian side started to classify casualties data and control the public debates.

During the Battle of Ilovaysk, relatives of the Ukrainian soldiers started public protests as they received information from the participants of the battle that they were being slaughtered. At least some part of these messages and the public actions were orchestrated by Russians. You can see how this influenced the next change in the information policy. The public picture and the regime of information accessibility for the Battle of Debaltseve was different, although the casualties were still numerous.

The Battles of Ilovaysk and Debaltseve were two major operations in the classical understanding of this term: battles where strategic planning and a significant number of troops were used by both sides. The remaining conflicts of the ATO/JFO were mostly on a tactical level. Unfortunately, both these battles were complete defeats for the Ukrainian Army.

In February 2015, the Minsk II Agreement was signed with the similar intention of political dialogue for peace. The ceasefire, however, was not kept by either side, and soon the conflict continued in a sporadic form. The failure of the Minsk Agreements was a topic for speculations on both sides of the conflict. Trying to engage in any kind of diplomacy angers the radical and militaristic part of society while continuing the conflicts slowly exhausts economic resources and brings "war fatigue."

Poroshenko was blamed by his opponents for the Minsk Agreements, both for the mentioned reasons and for its eventual failure. Unfortunately, the peace initiative of his successor was a failure as well. Another important fact about Poroshenko and his policy was the corruption scandals, especially concerning military industry.

Despite being an experienced diplomat and manager as well as keeping the course of nation-centered politics, Petro Poroshenko was mentioned in many anti-corruption investigations. The biggest scandals included those connected to supply contracts for the military industry, which had a huge media impact.

Was Poroshenko that corrupt? It is evident that a thorough "black PR" campaign was conducted against the President. Still, many investigations raised undeniable facts about corruption in the Ukrainian government. Unfortunately, his successors were not better in this respect.

Another military event that should be mentioned is the fight for the Donetsk airport. It started near the beginning of the campaign and in different forms and phases continued to January 2015 when Ukraine withdrew its forces from the facility. This battle had a huge media impact in Ukrainian society. For months, news from the airport was the main news for the whole state.

In fact, the battle became a real political myth. Ukrainian society perceived the fight as a heroic struggle in which the minority of the Ukrainian forces successfully opposed huge masses of enemy troops. The participants in that battle were called "cyborgs" — a name that originated from one of the Internet stories about the resilience of the defenders of the airport.

Criticism about these events, however, also exists. Separatists usually claim that the only reason the airport was not taken was that they never really put an effort into a battle of no strategic value. Fellow Ukrainian soldiers sometimes also criticize the myth. It is not completely understood why such a huge chunk of media attention was given to the Donetsk Airport Battle when there was an even fiercer battle at the Kramatorsk airport and, during 2015, intense fighting in Avdiivka.

It seems that the sense of these events again lies in the nature of "the media" and its role in contemporary armed conflicts. Media portrayal of that battle was an important factor in public opinion about the conflict, and, of course, it was useful to "feed the myth" even if it was originally created for propaganda.

Until February 2017, the conflict continued with occasional clashes until the escalation of the fighting near Avdiivka. A new group of consultants was assembled to revisit the Minsk II Agreement, but no real progress was achieved, unfortunately. A similar situation was set up for 2018.

On April 30, 2018, the Anti-Terrorist Operation was officially renamed the Joint Forces Operation. The aim was to change the emphasis on the context of the operation for public opinion. Before the Battle of Ilovaysk, officials had stated that the Donbass conflict might be resolved by force in a few weeks or months. In 2018, however, it was understood that the conflict was transforming into a "frozen" conflict.

The next big event in the history of the country was the 2019 presidential election. Petro Poroshenko wanted to have a second term and was ready for a PR and political fight for it. After a tense and hard struggle, a new president of Ukraine was elected: Volodymyr Zelensky, a former comedian, actor, and stand-up artist. Zelensky's background was his advantage; people were tired of war and corruption. Two of the main points of his election campaign were a promise to "talk with Putin" and finally achieve peace as well as to deal with corruption.

Nevertheless, he failed to fulfill his promise. There were ceasefires but never a new diplomatic solution and political reintegration of Donbass. This "peace program" was completely abolished in the beginning of 2022 with a full-scale Russian invasion. It is also doubtful that the situation with corruption in the government became any better. Indeed, there were significant changes in the public image and policy of the president as a result of the events connected to the conflict in Donbass.

Paradoxically, while Zelensky started his political career as a "fighter for peace" in contrast with Poroshenko (who held a quasi-militaristic nationalistic position in his policy of Donbass conflict), now Zelensky is even more militaristic. He indeed tried for the diplomatic solution, but it seems that the situation at the frontline was too complicated both morally and politically for any simple solution. This, however, is already a topic after 2022, and it does not concern this book.

The last important events of 2020 and 2021 concern the COVID pandemic and the escalation of the tensions on the Ukraine-Russia border. The pandemic is a historical event, but it does not concern the politics of the separate country directly. The healthcare policy employed at the period was indeed global and interesting for a historian, but it is doubtful that it is significant in comparison with the events of the UPR period. As for the escalation, we already know what consequences it wrought. Ukraine suffered a full-scale invasion that "nullified" the political state of the region, thereby making everything before February 2022 history.

There are a lot of similarities between the two time periods — armed conflicts, some of the diplomatic subtleties, and a lot of interesting historical and political figures. And there are differences, of course, which makes the problem of comparative analysis even more interesting.

The Ukrainian People's Republic period belongs to a different epoch not only in terms of technology. The society and the ideas guiding it were utterly different from their contemporary counterparts. Let us take some vivid examples. Socialism was a completely new thing for most of the population, which defined many of the unfolding historical events.

Today, we view socialism through the lens of the 70 years of experience of the Soviet Union. Of course, it has a completely different historical context. Socialism is just an example of the differences between the epochs. There are a lot of such differences between today's society and the UPR, each making the straightforward comparative analysis difficult. Still, comparative analysis does not mean that there should be only similarities between two phenomena.

Nevertheless, the similar details include structure-defining events and processes. Both periods had to deal with a revolution, the social and economic instability caused by it, and armed conflict. Both periods were marked by the struggle of cultures existing together and tensions within the society. These structure-defining elements make the idea of the comparative analysis rational and interesting. If the historical structures of the periods are similar with differences in details, then those differences are problematic and interesting to study.

The guiding methodological idea as stated in the previous chapter is empathetic analysis of the historical events and building a bigger picture based on that data. Both bigger pictures and "microhistories" will be compared not only for scientific interest, but also for identifying new political solutions to the actual problems of Ukrainian society.

3. Bolshevik Soviet Russia and Putin's Russia

To understand the Donbass conflict and the period between 2013 and 2022 in Ukraine, we should understand, to a certain extent, political processes that happened in the neighboring country of Russia. And for the UPR period, we need to know about Russia's historical counterpart—Soviet Russia—as well as about socialist and communist ideas in general.

The immediate questions raised are "in what way is contemporary Russia a legacy of the Soviet Union and what are the main differences between those two countries?" These details will also change the context for the described events in Ukraine. The analysis here is similar to the central idea of the book.

As is the case with contemporary Ukraine, the main contextual defining event for contemporary Russia is the collapse of the Soviet Union. It wrought all the previously described problems (e.g., poverty, unemployment, and corruption) to the central region of the former empire as well. Some of those problems were mitigated by the metropole status, whereas others were more severe than in the other former members of the Soviet Union. Organized crime, for example, was a particularly complex problem for the new Russian society.

The first president of the newly formed Russian Federation was Boris Yeltsin. He was a very interesting, charismatic figure. His policy was liberal, and his presidency was marked with many economic and political reforms. Not all of them, however, were successful. Some brought a lot of new problems, especially those connected to economics and corruption. Many people lost their savings and prestigious jobs and had to live in poverty due to the rapid transition to the open liberal market. Yeltsin was also often criticized for acquiring a huge wealth and creating a "close circle" of oligarchs who used their business privileges to acquire the same wealth. What is more, in the chaotic first years of transition to the new type of market, many people with a very doubtful reputation became wealthy and powerful members of society, which is still an irritating factor for the simple Russians.

In 1993, members of the Duma tried to overthrow Yeltsin. They blamed him and his government as well as the "shock therapy" economic reforms for the pervasive social problems described above. The conflict lasted for several days. President Yeltsin had to use military forces to stop the riot. There were casualties on both sides.

Another very questionable but important episode of Yeltsin's presidency is the First Chechen War. This small republic proclaimed its independence after the collapse of the Soviet Union, which created tensions between it and the Russian government that resulted in war in 1994–96. The conflict was very bloody with a lot of devastation and violations of human rights from both sides. The conflict was, in fact, lost by Russia. Chechnya gained de facto independence with the ambiguous status of an autonomous region of the Russian Federation.

Due to the outlined problems, Yeltsin started to lose popularity among the simple citizens. Most of the population was disappointed with the new reality, the economic situation, and the lost war. Meanwhile, the new presidential election campaign was planned for 1996.

Yeltsin was elected for a second term due to an extremely effective second election campaign (he was aided by an international team of experts). Most people were ready to vote for the communist leader. It is speculated that Yeltsin actively used election fraud during the campaign. Surprisingly, near the end of his second term, Boris Yeltsin recorded a famous statement about his resignation from his post and left Vladimir Putin as his successor.

At that time, Putin was not a famous public figure. A former KGB agent, he worked in the Saint-Petersburg's mayor's office after the collapse of the Soviet Union. His boss was Anatoly Sobchak—a famous politician who was blamed for ties with organized crime and had a somewhat strange death.

Putin's biographers often emphasize his role in Sobchak's administration as sort of a "fixer," thereby implying corruption and the same ties with the mafia. After some time and growth in ranks, Putin became a prime minister under Yeltsin. He still mostly remained in the shadow of the president, and his appointment was completely unexpected.

What was Russia in 1999? The shard of a great Empire, still possessing a lot of military and economic strength but slowly suffocating due to extensive corruption and the changed financial balance in the world. Organized crime is still a problem, although not as big as in the preceding period, but the mafia still has a "vote" in society.

The public opinion had two poles. Many people blamed liberal reforms and capitalism for corruption and poverty and dreamed of a return to Soviet power and stability. These people form the conservative and mostly militaristic part of the society and would provide strong support for Putin in the future, especially in the Donbass conflict problem.

The opposite pole were those who embraced liberal reforms and tried to find their place in the situation of the open market. These were usually people with higher education and intellectuals or people who wanted to be entrepreneurs. This group is an absolute minority, and in recent years, they have been persecuted for political actions. It can be characterized as the liberal opposition inside Russian society.

There were two major military conflicts on the territory of the Chechen Republic that tried to gain independence. The first conflict was lost by Yeltsin. The second conflict happened with Putin in power and was won. The historical context of the Second Chechen War involves acts of terrorism and conspiracy theories concerning these acts of terrorism.

Most of the society, however, appreciated Putin's measures against the separatists. It brought him a reputation as a strong, authoritarian, militaristic leader, whom he actually is, mostly. The political myth of Vladimir Putin was beginning to be forged.

Putin built his public image as an extremely strong, masculine type of leader who concentrates efforts on regaining Russia's lost place among the world's most powerful countries. In this pursuit for lost glory, this leader will not stop before physically destroying his enemies, even on the territory of other countries.

During the first years of his reign, Putin started to slowly gain control of the major media outlets until he reached the phase of no real freedom of speech in the Russian Federation. All the big media outlets support the official agenda, and the opposition has only less popular or even unofficial media channels, which are often subject to further political persecutions.

The Russian president is also known for several scandals concerning journalists who were working against him or his close associates. The most famous cases are the murders of Anna Politkovskaya, Natalia Estemirova, and Paul Klevbnikov. People who investigate the biography of the hypothetical schemes of Vladimir Putin are "on the radar" of FSS and other persecutory organs. There is no direct evidence, but all such cases look suspicious and are an object for scrutiny for international journalists.

Another famous murder is that of Alexander Litvinenko. He was a former intelligence officer who officially condemned Putin for corruption and using the FSS's resources to not only destroy personal enemies but also acquire personal wealth. Litvinenko had to emigrate to London, where, in 2006, he was poisoned with radioactive material and died.

In the first phase of Putin's coming to power, there were many quite influential players who wanted to challenge him for leadership. One was a billionaire, Mykhail Hodorkovski. His role during Yeltsin's presidency was at the top of the society, and his political influence was enormous. This makes his eventual fate symptomatic. In 2003, he was arrested on criminal charges and given a long prison sentence. His business empire was destroyed, and he was made an example of what happens to people who are against the government.

At least in the first years of his government, Putin won over those who opposed him. The social and economic structure of Russian society started to change drastically as compared to its time under Yeltsin. According to most of the economists, high prices for oil buoyed the economy of Russia as a serious power in geopolitics again. The balance of inequality shifted closer to acceptable.

The reasons for the serious strengthening of Russia over the last two decades, however, remains a topic for speculation and propaganda. The official position is that the strict policy of Vladimir Putin broke Russia's role as a neo-colony and established the order and stability that allowed for economic growth. Those who oppose the regime usually emphasize the accidental nature of this change and claim that since no real investments in social programs and high technology industries were made, the degradation of the economy will bring another shift in prices for natural resources.

Putin, as was mentioned previously, started and successfully won the Second Chechen War. The beginning of the second campaign was connected to several acts of terrorism committed in the central regions of the Russian Federation. In this way, officials saw the war as a war on terror.

There are some conspiracy theories connecting the FSS to the terrorist acts. The hypothesis is that the acts were plotted by the government to unify the nation and restore military influence. Nevertheless, there is no direct evidence and only speculation.

The short war between Russia and Georgia in 2008 is also worth mentioning to see a bigger picture. Russia was a long-time supporter of two regions, Abkhazia and South Ossetia, that proclaimed independence from Georgia in the 1990s. The relations between Georgia and these two new, little countries were quite tense with episodes of escalating violence.

In August 2008, Georgia invaded South Ossetia. There was an immediate response from the Russian Federation. Russian troops quickly pushed Georgian soldiers from the region and were ready for an offensive operation on the territory of Georgia when the ceasefire was negotiated on August 12, 2008.

Though very fast, this conflict was very important for international politics in the region as well as global politics. This was the first major conflict since the end of the Cold War where one side was supported by Russia and the other side by mostly the Western world. In fact, it was a classic "proxy" conflict from the Soviet era.

This proxy conflict marked a new period in Putin's policy. The message was sent to the global community that Russia had, to a certain extent, regained its imperial ambitions. According to the official position, Russia was protecting their ally and the Russian-speaking community. A similar position would be stated in the case of the Donbass conflict.

The Russian Federation also conducts military operations in Syria and some countries of Central Africa. Some of the operations are conducted directly by military forces and some through such proxy military forces as the notorious Wagner Group and other private military companies. The influence of the Russian Federation cannot be compared to that of Soviet Union, but it is still a regional leader, especially in Eastern Europe.

Much that is important can be said about the relations between Russia and China. China tends to be one of the few countries that can surpass the United States of America in economics. In recent years, the international relations between China and the USA have become a topic for many debates. Will China invade Taiwan? What will be the US response to that? Will there be a new world war? Will it be a nuclear war?

As for now, two new global superpowers are continuing the Cold War in the new contexts. Despite the numerous political and diplomatic tensions between the USA and China, their economic systems are connected so tightly that you can almost call them interdependent. They use local conflicts of the proxy powers as games to decide little shifts in global political influence. The race in high-technology weapons, IT, and other technology continues but in a different way than during Soviet times.

Everything, however, can change drastically in a very short period of time. Many people connect this probable change to the future situation with Taiwan. Ukraine's "situation" is also important because it is one of the described proxy conflicts through which the two sides probe each other.

In different phases of Putin's rule, there have been different policies, including the international policy especially connected to Ukraine and Eastern Europe. During Yeltsin's presidency, there was still a big influence and connection between the two countries. Russia still saw itself as the "elder brother," but the relations were much more liberal.

Putin began his international policy as you could expect from this leader — in a much more authoritarian way. Ukraine and other former Soviet republics were now a sphere of direct geopolitical interest for the Russian Federation. This included the financial support of pro-Russian political candidates as well as intelligence services operations in these countries.

As was mentioned in the previous chapter, Leonid Kuchma tried to strike a balance in relations with the West and the Russian Federation. When the crisis that included the murder of Gongadze broke out, it became almost impossible. Most of the western countries declared Kuchma an unwanted person, and he had to lean toward Russia.

That crisis was one of the presupposing details of the next crisis in 2004. The Orange Revolution and its consequences were mostly described in the previous chapter. It is also important to mention the reaction of the Russian Federation to that event.

At that time, Kuchma, because of the mentioned reasons, supported the strengthening of ties with the northern neighbor. Yanukovich, as a candidate, was negotiated previously with Putin and was supported by official representatives of the Russian Federation.

In his election campaign, Viktor Yanukovich made a lot of promises concerning strengthening ties with Putin's Russia — both cultural and economic. Had he won, Ukraine probably would have become much like today's Belarus — a satellite country.

It is useful to mention again that this big choice between Russia and the West would play a great role in the Revolution of Dignity. In 2004, Yanukovich eventually lost the second elections. Nevertheless, pro-Russian forces negotiated the constitutional changes, and, after Viktor Yushchenko came to power, played a crucial role in his eventually lost struggle for control and the return of Yanukovich.

The public image of the Orange Revolution in Russia was severely negative. It was represented as a nationalistic, quasi-fascist rebellion that denied the result of the democratic election. It was emphasized that regions like Donbass and Crimea would be oppressed both culturally and economically during Yushchenko's term in office.

Pro-Russian political parties in Ukraine are heavily financially supported by Russia. After Putin gained political power, this "soft power" influence became a priority for the Russian Federation. Russians say the same "soft power" is applied in the Eastern Europe region by NATO and the USA. The same old controversy.

During the years immediately following his coming to power, Vladimir Putin was systematically strengthening his apparatus and modelling his authoritarian regime after that of the late Soviet Union. For a certain time, Dmitry Medvedev became the president and Putin the prime minister. All the key decisions, however, were still made by Putin, and the final goal was to allow the latter to be elected for two new terms.

Yanukovich was mostly an ally to Putin, but there were a lot of patriotic forces in Ukrainian society that were open adversaries to Russian culture and the international policy of Vladimir Putin. The conflict with Ukraine became especially deep in 2013-14 when the Revolution of Dignity began. This event, as well as the following annexation of Crimea made with the profound help of Russian military forces, was described in the previous chapter.

Russian Federation officials blamed the Maidan activists for the illegal coup just as in the 2004 Orange Revolution. Only this time, there were no negotiations for changes to the Constitution. Russia took radical measures instead — annexation of Crimea and support for Strelkov's armed groups.

Maidan's revolutionaries were seen as radical nationalists, even fascists, who provoked riot police and military. The policemen from Berkut and other special forces were seen as heroes. The new government of Petro Poroshenko was explicitly referred to as a "military junta." Russian propagandists blamed the new government for all the "sins" of independent Ukraine, like corruption, inequality, and high crime rates, as well as new sins, including racism, language chauvinism, and support of NATO expansion.

Russia officially supported the usage of Russian language in Ukraine and numerous events connected to the popularization of

Russian culture as well as cultural ties with Ukraine in particular. The question of language remains quite important here. Putin declared that one of the main aims of his military operations in Ukraine is to protect the Russian-speaking part of the population.

It is probably worth mentioning that now, after February 2022, the connection between Russian and Ukrainian culture has become even more complicated. The remaining ties are being severed, and the Ukrainian language is becoming more and more widely used in Ukrainian society. For the first time in the history of the country, Russian-affiliated culture has become a sort of underground culture. It is an interesting question: what result will this culture war bring in the future?

So, what was Russia as a country in 2014–22? First of all, it was a country headed by a very strong authoritarian leader with a nationalistic agenda. The country was once one of the most powerful empires on the planet, which fostered nostalgia for that imperial past in a majority of the population.

The Russian Federation, as with all countries with such a past, is chauvinistic toward other cultures (i.e., it is not only about Ukraine). And especially so when it comes to the minor countries with independent national cultures. Russians see themselves as people who can bring those countries their civilization and the usage of the Russian language as a bridge for international communication.

Of course, there are all the classic "minuses" to that imperial policy, like the slow degradation of the national culture under the influence of metropole, colonial economic status, and everyday chauvinism. It is no surprise many people are against metropole control. The way to fight it is to develop and propagate national culture. That is why there is a schism in Ukrainian society.

There are no easy solutions to this conflict. At its core, it is the same empire-colony conflict that has been present on the globe since the Roman Empire. It is even worse now in the modern, globalized world. Apart from the past dilemmas, it is also about the fundamental choice of the individual between Western and Eastern values and policy.

There are fully independent national cultures in the world today. During Soviet times, to be a nationalist-affiliated dissident automatically meant you mostly supported the Western World. Metropole culture, even in the form of the scholar's work, was voted on by the policy of metropole. This situation made conspiracy theorists speculate that there are actually no national cultures in small countries anymore, only specific ways to vote for the global West—this is similar to the situation described with "Bismarck's Plan."

Russian political scientists and thinkers, for their part, claim that Ukraine is much more of a colony for the West in today's situation. The controversy again concerns values and political ideas as well as the general worldview. It seems that, at least on the ideological side of things, the struggle for Ukraine is ever persistent.

Nevertheless, what was the status of Soviet Russia, a historical counterpart of Putin's Russia, and what is the relation between these two historical periods? We, of course, can view only a very limited period of time, namely 1917–22. This was the youth of communism when Vladimir Lenin was still in power. This period of Soviet Russia is special because there were many new ideas and not all the traditional features of the regime were present. Some things, however, will be said about the later period and its connection to today's Russia as well.

The Soviet Union was a unique political regime that performed many global experiments on the economic and social structure of society. Some were successful, but many others brought unforeseen, sometimes-catastrophic consequences for the lives of simple people. The regime was also persecuting all who were against it, even those who did not engage in the armed resistance. Extensive persecution of the opposition in the Stalin era was one of the most tragic moments in the history of the 20th century. The continuing persecution in some of the later years was still a savage violation of the human rights of the citizens of the country. Lenin had no such total and systematic policy as Stalin later did, but during his rule many enemies of the Soviet Union also ended up persecuted.

During the time of the UPR, the "Soviet project" was only beginning to emerge. The social basis for it was a powerful socialist underground movement in tsarist Russia. The Russian Empire at that time was mostly a failed state. Inequality, social and economic conflicts, corruption, and absence of reforms were slowly eating at this once powerful country from the inside.

The previous chapter described the catastrophic military defeat in war with Japan as well as the profoundly ineffective actions on the Eastern Front of the First World War. Nevertheless, they were just the symptoms. The political system of the Empire was too archaic to solve the new problems and issues. The Russian Empire could not cope with the national movements inside the country, including the Ukrainian national movement. It likewise could not cope with the even more powerful socialist movement that stemmed from the social inequality and deep poverty of proletarians and peasants.

The political police of the Russian Empire persecuted the participants in the socialist movement. They were imprisoned, hanged, or sent to Siberia. Socialists agitated among the citizens, organized protests and strikes, and sometimes committed acts of terrorism. Many socialists were in exile abroad, where they formed a powerful diaspora, trained their organizational skills, and discussed ideology while waiting for the right moment to return to Russia and start a full-scale Revolution. One of them was future communist idol and the leader of the Russian Revolution, Vladimir Lenin.

Eventually, the moment came. The First World War was a catastrophic event for the state, and socialist-oriented enemies of the regime decided to use it for the project of the Revolution. During wartime, a main factor of destabilization was communist agitators, both among the soldiers on the front and among the proletariat inside the country. Left-wing political activists demanded an end to the war, which they considered to be imperialistic, and the overthrow of the tsarist government to build a completely new society.

Nevertheless, pro-socialist powers inside Russian society were not alone in striving for changes. There were people who wanted liberal reforms, conservative and militaristic forces that thought that this particular tsar was incompetent, aristocrats who wanted to restore the Duma without further radical changes that concerned the tsar, etc.

It is indeed true that the socialists were the most supported faction due to their enormous popularity among simple citizens. There was, however, a huge social basis for revolution among all classes of society. There were so many problems in the Russian Empire that there were people at all levels who felt that changes were needed. This is precisely why Lenin and other communists called the situation in the Russian Empire "pre-revolutionary." Instability and chaos was considered the best time for quick revolt and profound changes in the structure of the society. Later events showed that communists were actually right in their analysis of the situation.

As was described in the previous chapter in the context of the international relations of the UPR, there were two consecutive revolutions in the Russian Empire—the February Revolution that established Kerensky's provisional government and the October Revolution, a revolt inside the revolt that established Vladimir Lenin and his radical communist government.

Lenin was a radical intellectual communist who built the government mechanism of one of the most closed societies in the history of humankind. At least in the first phase of his rule, Lenin was an orthodox Marxist who viewed Russia as a starting ground for the radical transformation of both the economy and the political model of the whole world.

Communist society denied private property and the economic relations that involve money. Soon after the October Revolution, the Red government tried to establish different economic relations in the society. Nevertheless, this model was very hard to implement, especially in the context of the ongoing war and a massive underground White Movement. There were numerous challenges for Lenin and the Party.

Eventually, the communist leader had to return to mostly monetary economic politics. The state was not ready for such a profound reform. Apart from that, there was the huge influence of the postwar situation—poverty and a ruined economy and social institutions. Communists had to do something to revive the economy.

The decision was made to implement a new course—New Economic Politics (NEP). NEP was a return to monetary relations and certain capitalist institutions in society. Peasants could sell their production, and established prices and small businesses (co-operatives) were allowed. NEP was a serious relief for the economy and simple citizens.

Nevertheless, it was a step back from the point of view of communist ideals. Lenin thought it was a necessary step back to grow the economy of the devastated country a little bit after which the profound reforms and the World's Revolution would continue. NEP was indeed canceled in the Stalin era. We already know that the World's Revolution never happened and that the followers of Joseph Stalin concentrated their efforts on building socialism in one separate country—Russia.

As was mentioned previously, in March 1918, Soviet Russia signed the Treaty of Brest-Litovsk with Germany that ended the fight on the Eastern Front and sacrificed a huge territory and vast resources to the Central Powers. However morally ambiguous it was in a political sense, it was also a very smart move for Lenin that let him consolidate power and cope with other challenges.

What was the ideology behind those maneuvers? The Party officially condemned the whole First World War as imperialistic—waged for colonial wealth, immoral, and violent. The only true war was the World's Revolution—the political struggle to establish socialism globally and build the communist society after.

Vladimir Lenin believed that socialism in Russia was only the first step for the worldwide revolution. Communist ideology was extremely popular around the world at that time. Even the United States had a communist political party that was popular enough. Soviet Russia would support all such movements around the world, especially those which concerned armed resistance against capitalism.

In this vein, Lenin and Russian communists supported the "red" movement in Ukraine. In this case, however, it is speculated that Ukrainian communists were never independent from Soviet Russia and their anti-UPR actions and revolt were orchestrated and supported by Russia. Compare this to the situation with the contemporary Russian Federation and the separatists in the Donbass region.

The fate of the separate Bolshevik Ukrainian party is symptomatic. Shortly after the end of the civil war, its key members were persecuted, and a little bit later, it was dismissed. Russian communists were loyal to the principle that there should be only one Party, only one guiding principle. Ukrainian "reds" were useful tools that were thrown away after they were used.

Apart from the Ukrainian national movement that was proclaimed to be a "bourgeois" enemy, one of the main challenges for Lenin was the White Movement. The White Movement consisted mainly of former aristocrats who were loyal to the tsar and tried to "save Russia." The biggest groups of the White Army were situated in Siberia, the Don river basin, and Crimea.

The relation between the UPR and the White movement in Crimea was complex. At a certain point, some of the diplomats of the Ukrainian People's Republic thought of uniting their forces with the Whites against the Bolsheviks, but the negotiations failed. The White Movement saw the UPR as rebels who should not be given a single bit more of autonomy. In fact, the White Movement was probably even more chauvinistic toward Ukrainian nationalism than the Bolsheviks.

In time, the White Army was completely defeated by the Red Army, and in 1922, the civil war officially ended. Many surviving members of the White Movement emigrated to Europe and other Western countries. The same fate awaited the surviving public figures of the UPR.

The Bolsheviks saw UPR emigration as a minor threat compared to the "Whites." The Soviet secret service, or Cheka, still paid attention to the Ukrainian diaspora. It is speculated that Petlura was murdered in Paris by a "Red" agent and not a simple vigilante. There were also counterintelligence operations within the borders of the state, mostly against intellectuals connected to the UPR culturally or politically.

So, what was Soviet Russia in the 1917–22 period? Despite being "a great experiment" in a sociopolitical sense, it still had a lot of features of its imperial past, including chauvinism toward cultures of the smaller nations. Although it lost giant territories, it was still a very big country with aims and the resources to regain everything it lost and conquer even more. It was an empire, and it would become an even greater empire with time.

Due to its ideology, Soviet Russia persecuted any kind of national movement, including the Ukrainian national movement, on an even bigger scale than the Russian Empire. In a sense, Cheka saw the UPR danger as another branch of the "bourgeoisie" of the White Movement.

Was Lenin's country already totalitarian? It is evident that it had a strong authoritarian leadership and overpowered organs of political persecution. Nevertheless, there were centers of alternative thought in the Party itself, some freedom of expression, and what is more important—the spirit of the time was different. Soviet Russia was, first of all, the greatest socialist experiment since the French Revolution.

Besides, totalitarianism includes many technical features: the totalization of the media, constant surveillance and the search for the enemy within, the unification of the education system, and strict control over any social activity of the citizens. Lenin was probably eager to use these methods for political control, but there was none of the required infrastructure for that in the country.

Stalin's Russia was indeed the product of the great social experiment, but its results were far from the initial expectations of the leaders of the Revolution. The USSR became one of the first totalitarian societies in the world and was full of paranoia and aggression. There was no inequality on the previous scale nor poverty and corruption. But the price for that was establishing absolutely inhumane social conditions of existence. No freedom, no choice, and an absolutely stagnant state of affairs in all spheres of life, including the domestic.

This was all the result of Lenin's failed experiment in 1917–22. Many would say that it is a sign of a moral bankruptcy of Vladimir Lenin and his Party, a fundamental corruption of his view on Marxist ideology that brought the unforeseen global consequences. That is debatable. In the context of this little research study, it is important to note what legacy early Soviet Russia left for its successor.

Is contemporary Russia so different from Soviet Russia in 1917–22? Despite having certain legacy features, it is very different. There is no "spirit of the great experiment" in Putin's Russia. In fact, this country follows the path of countries that were accused of imperialism by Lenin. Today's Russia has a very strong national culture, which it uses to suppress the other narratives and dominate its satellites. It extensively uses military force not for the purposes of revolution and establishing justified social order but for the protection of the dominant culture. This is how empires build their policy.

In fact, in the contemporary context, and especially in the case of the Donbass armed conflict, the Russian Federation is much more like the tsarist Russian Empire. Just like the tsarist Russian Empire, the Russian Federation devotes vast economic resources to regional conflicts and to support regional control while not giving enough attention to such severe internal problems as corruption and inequality.

As for the period after February 2022, the Russian Federation is bearing more resemblance to the Soviet Union of Stalin's rule. Persecutions are becoming more and more harsh and country wide. The propaganda rhetoric is already at a historical peak and sending the message about a new struggle with the western world and even a possible nuclear war. Leaders of public opinion claim the special mission of the nation and the need to search for enemies within.

As for the technical infrastructure required for mass surveillance and governmental control over every aspect of the private lives of citizens—today's Russia has even greater capabilities than its predecessor. There is only one little step remaining for the Russian Federation on the path to a totalitarian state. That is the ideological positioning of the state as the ultimate goal of every citizen's activity and the corresponding changes in the social structure of the society. The process connected to this has already begun.

Yet Putin and his policy would have been impossible without a Soviet past. Imperialism, chauvinism, militarism, and negation of international law grow from the political worldview of Lenin and his followers. These are all features that formed into today's shape during the late periods of the Soviet Empire, but the foundation was laid in 1917.

Vladimir Lenin and his supporters gave the Ukrainian People's Republic no chance. Their initial peaceful initiatives were just a masquerade while they were trying to suppress the national movement through political tools rather than military force. When the political solution failed, the Bolsheviks used their military capabilities.

In the view of the Reds, the UPR was a bourgeoisie and a chauvinistic society, just the type of society that produces the ruling minority of the super-rich and poor general population. They saw all the inequality of the Russian Empire doubled in the young Ukrainian state. Propaganda portrayed UPR officials as a gang of thieves who only existed due to the help of the Central Powers. The term "fascism" was not widely used in those days, but it is pretty evident that the Bolsheviks considered the UPR one of its prime enemies, fascists. The tensions between the two states even worsened after Simon Petlura came to power.

Putin's Russia views today's Ukraine as a Nazi state. Ukrainian nationalists are proclaimed aggressive nazi followers, and the development of the national culture is just a disguise for the virulent propaganda that is supported by the world's fascist community. Ukrainian ethnos as a separate identity does not exist and is, in fact, an artificial construct to weaken and corrupt Russia. In the eyes of Vladimir Putin, Zelensky and Poroshenko are fake, the real administration of Ukraine is the internationally appointed military junta, etc.

In this way, despite the deep differences between the Soviet and Russian societies, there is a Bolshevik legacy perceived by the contemporary Russian Federation that resulted in its pro-imperial politics that, in turn, resulted in the Donbass conflict and the later invasion of 2022.

However debatable all these positions are, it is important to understand the ideological part of Russian society while in the struggle with Putin and the forces that he represents. The same is true about the UPR period and Soviet Russia.

4. Contemporary Ideological Debates

In the previous chapters, the question of ideology was raised several times. Ideology is a big chunk of the history of society, especially in the 20th century. It is impossible to assess the so-called hybrid war without taking this factor into consideration because ideology as well as media campaigns are a big part of such a conflict. The events of 1917–22 also involved a lot of ideology, including the socialism-versus-capitalism debate and the question of Ukrainian nationalism. And there are, of course, as this research project presupposes, analogies between the two periods that can be analyzed.

Ukrainian nationalism concerns the set of problems around Ukrainian identity. Does a separate Ukrainian identity exist? Russians often claim that, actually, it does not. In their view, Ukrainian language is, at best, a dialect of Russian polluted by Polish influence, and the whole history of Ukraine is just a branch of Russian history, the history of the southern regions of the Russian Empire. This was stated in the previous chapters.

Ukrainians try to disprove such a position both by taking part in the debates around the issues and creating authentic national culture. Any work of art that concerns national identity is a powerful argument in this great debate.

In this way, any serious Ukrainian culture artifact—from books to work of art—also bears a political message and a political context. And the Ukrainian artist or scholar is often a political figure, a participant in the political debate. This is sometimes a reason why Ukrainian culture is deemed dependent on politics and inferior to cultures that can exist without an obligatory political context.

Is that really so? Contemporary art is often included in politics, and the classic art is always a part of national identity and cultural heritage, especially in the case of Ukraine. Historical circumstances define the identity-related ideological struggles in Ukrainian society. Does an ironic element in the synthesis of culture and politics define its status as "high" or "low"? In any case, the question of the relations between the culture and national politics is more of philosophy. It cannot be established that it is a minus for Ukrainian culture for certain.

Moreover, mixing art and culture with politics is often a trend in the intellectual life of modern society. It was the case in Soviet Russia in the 1920s, and it is often the case in Western countries nowadays. From another point of view, such mixing is also a sign of a closed society, especially when without irony. This was often the case when radical poets-politicians in some of the young communist regimes transformed into pure political radicals.

It should be mentioned that the debates around all these and connected questions seem to be eternal. They will continue as long as Ukraine and Russia in this or that form exist. These debates, however, are extremely important for the politics of the region. Revolutions, military clashes, and other catastrophic events were often triggered by these old debates about language, identity, history, etc. Every historical monograph on these questions is viewed not only scientifically but also ideologically.

What is hybrid war? Today, after the full-scale invasion, this term is not that popular anymore. Nevertheless, during the conflict in Donbass in 2014–22, it was often used to describe the situation. Russia never declared an official war on Ukraine. It never admitted its troops on the territory of the neighboring country, and it mostly used proxy military groups as well as black ops. In a hybrid conflict, media coverage and ideology are used not only to support the military operations, but also as a valuable part of the campaign. All this is consistent with what was predicted by Baudrillard.

Old debates are becoming even more "weaponized" in this context. The struggle of ideas was already tense in the UPR, but, with the growth of media and communication technologies, it also grew. Ideology and humanities are the part of the informational campaign that is vital warfare for each side of the conflict. Simple citizens are overwhelmed by the different signals and content that surrounds them in contemporary situations. Are we Ukrainians? Are we Russians? Was the Soviet Union a justified society? Is being a part of Europe indeed our identity? Is siding with Ukraine equal to siding with fascists? Or is it Putin who is a real new Nazi?

Questions of all sorts about the socioeconomic system are also quite pressing. Is socialism a more advanced worldview than capitalism? Does capitalism mean freedom of thought and prosperity? Is it even moral to live in a capitalistic society after the period of the Soviet Union? Is nationalism of any form moral?

All these controversies, in addition to the historical debates, are described in the previous chapter (e.g., debates about Kievan Rus', Mazepa, the UPR, etc.). Special attention is given to the Second World War, thereby implying that the contemporary sociopolitical situation in Eastern Europe is mostly defined by this exact global conflict.

Some debaters have an extremely solid opinion that will never change no matter the surrounding signals. But such people are in the absolute minority. Most of the population is influenced by media and authoritative figures. Winning the hearts of the population is half of the success in the contemporary war. Hence why, apart from the military campaigns, there are literal propaganda clashes in the media.

It is also useful to view these issues in a more global picture. Due to its geography and historical context, Ukraine is between two giant geopolitical spheres of influence—Europe and the East. While the opposition of these two sides continues, our country will be the battlefield not only for military forces but also for ideology and conflicting values.

Russia, in this way, is a representative of the East. The closest ideas that appear in the mind when thinking about this connection are paternalism, traditionalism, collective social values, and strong appeal to Orthodox Christianity in its Muscovite form.

Russian propagandists usually claim that those are features of a special form of the high spirituality of the Russian nation in particular. This spirituality defines a very special role for Russia as a country that bridges East and West, a chosen nation with a special mission and path of historical evolution.

The idea of a special path goes back to the Russian religious philosophers of the second half of the 19th century. Russian identity and connected spirituality were at the center of their many works. The idea of an imperial Russia, a country that can use military force against its neighbors to restore order and balance, has even deeper historical roots.

These imperial ideas were foreign in the early days of Russian statehood under the influence of the conflict with both the western and eastern civilizations. Ukrainian historians often emphasize the eastern influence, in particular, as the factor that sowed the future conflict with Ukraine, which is more influenced by the West.

Nevertheless, most Russian ideologists do not consider eastern influence a disadvantage. Instead, they concentrate their criticism around Ukrainian identity and claim that it is Western culture that is, in fact, completely alien to the Slavic nation.

Are all these media and propaganda messages indeed reflecting Russian society and its conflicts with its neighbors? It is not only Ukrainian media in the counterpropaganda campaign that claim that, actually, no, they are not. Putin's Russia is aggressive toward minorities and militaristic and ambitious toward new lands and spheres of influence, but there are no signs that it represents a special spirituality. Instead, it is really oppressive toward people of culture as well as scientists.

Foreign policy that seeks more and more influence and wealth (which is precisely the case in the contemporary Russian Federation) is a classic imperial stance. Such a stance defines the moral status of such societies as well. Empires and aggressive states, in general, are not about spirituality or a "special path."

A lot was said about the Soviet Union, its history and collapse, and the impact on the contemporary situation, especially in the context of international relations between Ukraine and Russia. But is the contemporary Russian Federation the same as the Soviet Union?

It is evident that the Soviet Union left a great legacy for the new Russia both in an economic and ideological sense. However, the politics and society of today's country is much more different than similar. Russia appeals to the Soviet experience and culture when it is about winning the hearts of the people, but, in fact, the

Russian Federation is much closer to the opposing regimes that existed in the early period of the Soviet Union.

It is the economy before all. Russians are playing on the world's capitalistic markets. The Soviet Union also sold its goods on the international level, but it was always in the mainstream of Lenin's ideology — only to gain political advantage over the opposing states. Wealth and financial resources are important indicators of the social status of a person in today's country, which is in direct contradiction of communist values.

Economics, and especially big business, are tightly connected to regional politics and security, which is, in fact, the classic feature of the fascist state. Mussolini and Hitler, despite their aggressive positions toward Bolshevism, actually borrowed the socialist ideology of market control instead of the free market. An alternative way of doing it — informal political influence rather than a formal planned economy — became characteristic of their regimes.

Hitler also used the planned economy at a certain phase. Political economy scholars often point to this as the detail that implies a close connection between fascism and radical communism. In this way, however, contemporary Russia is closer to fascist Italy.

Despite the mentioned appeal to Soviet culture, Putin and his followers have a somewhat ambiguous attitude toward socialism and communism. The concentration of power and wealth by the Russian elite is all thanks to the open market economy. The rules of the game were corrupt and anti-liberal, but this would never have happened in the communist society. Contemporary communists are also one of the few forces in Russian society that have enough support to be considered an alternative to the official political system. This can often be perceived as a danger by the established political elite.

In fact, communism in its classic form is antagonistic toward what is happening in Putin's Russia today. The Russian Federation relies more on the cultural messages of traditional society and collective values. It cannot coexist with such advanced communist concepts as internationalism, social equality, and controlling the market.

To sum up—the Russian Federation is a completely different society from that of the Soviet Union. They are, however, still connected by legacy-successors relations. This was mostly stated in the previous chapter, but it is useful to recall key moments to draw two new conclusions: the Russian Federation is not actually a pro-socialist or pro-communist state, and it is only using the glamor of the Soviet Union's ideology to recruit followers.

Then how about the ideas of contemporary Russian ideologists? The mentioned paternalism and traditionalism? The official position of the Russian Federation is support for the traditional family as well as the conservative schema of the coexistence of the simple citizens and the major social institutions. This is, by the way, again very similar to the details of fascist political systems.

This traditional view on things is different today than it was in 1991 because of the context of new trends in the West, especially the LGBTQ communities and gender studies advanced in the USA and Europe both in theory and the practical defense of the rights of those communities. The Russian Federation officially chooses to oppose those trends to "protect" the traditional family, which brings to its cause many supporters in Eastern Europe and Asia.

Even if you vote for traditional values, however, Russia may not be the best option for political support. It is evident to any educated person that Russian Federation leaders do not care much for traditional values, or morality in general, and their oppressive actions are just means to fulfill the political program. And that political program, especially in most recent years, is getting closer to a strong authoritarian government and neofascist ideology. Meanwhile, fascism, in any form, is the most morally corrupt social order.

What about the West and western values? Another pole of this great debate is Europe and the United States of America. Joining the European Union and becoming part of the international community is proclaimed as one of the main goals of all the pro-national political parties in Ukraine. Pro-European rhetoric and ideology has become especially popular since the presidential campaign of 2004 and entered the mainstream of the government's ideology in 2014, after Maidan. Sharing European values and fighting the corruption as well as external enemies is stated as the way to enter the international community for the young country.

The Russian point of view on the situation is completely different, of course. The European Union will never accept Ukraine as an equal partner or even with the status of "younger brother." The whole, separate Ukrainian identity is an ideological trick invented to weaken Russian and Asian influence in Ukrainian society. The West just does not take Ukraine and its people seriously. In fact, joining the European Union in any form would be accepting the status of a neo-colony. After that, Ukrainians will be objects for all sorts of oppression and exploitation.

According to Russian propaganda, European society is morally flawed and inherently evil. The great victory in World War 2 was achieved due to the colossal sacrifice of Soviet people and their heroism, but, despite the efforts to denazify Europe, it still remains secretly loyal to Hitler's ideology. In fact, contemporary European society is a direct heir to the Third Reich with all its features: racism, irrational greed, and moral quietism when it comes to oppression of ethnic minorities.

Corruption is the basic feature of any capitalistic society. It is impossible to fight it without rebuilding the whole society according to new rules. The measures against corruption taken in Ukraine nowadays are, in fact, just a media campaign that is used to destroy opponents' political reputation and introduce foreign administrative structures into all the processes inside the country.

The new trend toward gender and sexual minorities was already mentioned. Although Adolf Hitler was also aggressively against LGBTQ, the Russian Federation modified its political ideology in the context of traditional values. The growth of the civil rights movement for sexual minorities is interpreted as the complete moral bankruptcy of the West and Europe in terms of spirituality and morality. Russia poises itself as the protector of traditionalism and morality in this way.

Taking all of this into consideration, it is very interesting to see how contemporary Russia blames Ukraine for "ultranationalism" and reviving Nazi ideology. In fact, that is one of the cornerstones of the Russian officials' ideological program toward the Donbass conflict. The Russian Federation, however, is similar to the classic fascist regimes not only in terms of economics, but also in terms of the ideas dominating in the society and its social hierarchy.

Virulent militarism in all spheres of life of the society as well as revanchism for the lost status of the Empire are the same factors that were present in the society of Hitler's Germany in the years preceding the Second World War. People affiliated with the military, police, and especially with the secret services, are actively glorified by the media, whereas intellectual elites and dissidents are consciously dehumanized and labeled as "passive enemies" of the state.

Of course, the Russian media draws a completely different picture of the relations between Ukraine and the Russian Federation. Ukraine as a state is indeed radicalized and mobilized by the events of 2014 and especially by the full-scale invasion of 2022. In this book, we mainly focus on the events of 2014–22. Nevertheless, some of the main trends of social life after February 2022 were already present in the preceding period.

Russia blames Ukrainian society for the rapid growth of different pro-nationalistic and even pro-Nazi organizations and paramilitary groups. Nationalism, however, was hardly the main trend for Ukrainian politics in the period before 2014. Political media coverage was mostly on the socioeconomic agenda. The trend for radical forms of nationalism began to form due to the catastrophic events of the Donbass conflict.

Was Ukrainian society in 2014 as radicalized as it was in 2011? Of course it was, but the main reason for this is a hybrid war and the ideological influence that accompanies it. Ukrainians understand nationalism and its ideology as an obligatory measure in face of pressure that may assimilate their identity.

It is indeed true that the form and the content of Ukrainian politics changed forever in 2014. Identity-related issues and national memory became dominant ideas in public policy instead of the aforementioned socioeconomic agenda. Corruption is still widely discussed, but now it is presented in a wider program of national policy. Corrupt politicians and officials are seen as the enemies of the state and people, an internal enemy.

In this way, economic crimes and economics in general are interpreted politically to become another tool for propaganda messages and psychological manipulation. That is, perhaps, not the best thing for the economy of the country but such are the circumstances. It is but another sign of the radicalization of the society.

Maidan and the events that followed mobilized the masses of the Ukrainian population just as during and after the French Revolution, military-affiliated activity became a social elevator and the only road to public politics for many simple citizens. Of course, not all of them were pure patriots, and some were just searching for social and financial profits. It is the nature of any revolution.

The role of the military, the historian, and the political analyst in Ukrainian society began to transform. The role of this particular scholar is intrinsically connected to identity and culture, and thus to the ideology of nationalism. This is especially vivid in the so-called decommunization campaign.

The decommunization campaign is a series of laws renaming local and global place names to get rid of the Soviet legacy in the culture and instead embrace the "roots" of the Ukrainian national identity. Pro-national forces had mentioned the importance of such a campaign since the 1990s, but it started only after the Maidan in 2014. The campaign became especially rapid after the full-scale invasion in 2022.

Pro-Russian and pro-Soviet historians claim that such a campaign is a violation of the cultural heritage and an attempt to rewrite history. They center their position around the myth about the Second World War, thereby implying that Ukrainians are trying to indirectly get rid of the memory of heroic Soviet soldiers and blur the crimes committed by the Nazi regime. Pro-Russian debaters also emphasize that western Ukrainian culture is alien to the central and eastern parts of the country such that there is actually no genuine memory of the Ukrainian national place names in those regions. The campaign, as well as the particular names, are the subjects of hot debates at the time of writing.

What about the period of the Ukrainian People's Republic? It also bore a severe ideological conflict. It is interesting to see how this period in the history of Ukraine is interpreted in contemporary Russia. This interpretation brings the keys to understanding both the old and the new conflicts.

First of all, Russian historians tend to interpret the whole UPR case as something minor as compared to the revolutions and the civil war. For contemporary Ukraine, the UPR and its founders are some of the main foundations of the national idea, whereas pro-Russian scholars usually claim that there was never a solid state and that it was rather a series of chaotic revolts on the territory of Ukraine when a few different armed gangs competed for power and influence. Then, the Bolsheviks came and restored order. It was just an episode of the Civil War, and the White Movement was far more important to Lenin.

This view both has the natural chauvinistic and the ideological aspect. You probably will not grant the "conquered tribe" a rich history because it is dangerous for the metropole. The "Bismarck's Plan" concept can be recalled here again in a slightly different light. If you acknowledge the strong culture, it becomes much harder to assimilate the inhabitants of the region. The UPR period, as viewed by Ukrainian historians, laid the foundations of the Ukrainian state and had many powerful figures and military leaders. The Russian view of things was already described.

UPR public figures in Ukraine are viewed as sometimes complex personalities who not only made a lot of mistakes, but also were heroes, builders of statehood, and the foundation for the future independence of the country. They are glorified by the media. Their lives and accomplishments are studied in schools and universities.

The Russian point of view is that they were mostly random people who were appointed to their places by Germans and Western diplomatic elites. After the support of those elites ceased, the UPR just collapsed. Soviet propaganda portrays Hrushevsky and other top officials almost as caricatures—incompetent, morally flawed, and sometimes idiotic. It is especially interesting to recite these views when it comes to the Ukrainian military leaders of that period.

Pavlo Skoropadsky, who is the ultimate military hero and leader of state in the eyes of Ukrainians, is considered by Russian historians like a scammer who decided to bet on Ukraine in times of chaos in the former empire. Skoropadsky was a Russian general who decided to raise his political status by participating in the project of a "banana republic." He was completely controlled by the Germans, and without their support, his own forces were worth nothing even against other factions inside the UPR.

Even worse is their understanding of Simon Petliura. Due to the questionable antisemitic acts committed on the territory of Ukraine, he is labeled an anti-Semite, an authoritarian leader, and a "bloody dictator". Most Ukrainian historians doubt that it was so plain and whether Petliura had influence over the mentioned antisemitic campaigns. He is also blamed for military crimes and incompetent leadership that caused the death of his own men. This public figure has a very interesting biography of becoming a military leader after participating in the sphere of culture for most of his life. Such a career trajectory, however, was typical for Hitler's Germany and Mussolini's Italy. In 1917–22, there was no term "fascism," but had there been, Soviet propaganda would obviously have labelled the UPR a fascist or protofascist state.

This is evident from how the later Soviet education system and popular culture (e.g., historical films) portrayed the UPR and its main public figures: The Ukrainian language is an unnatural construct that is used only for ideological reasons. Ukrainian national culture is primitive and artificial and used mostly for the same purposes. UPR leaders were idiots, scammers, and criminals who started the whole "Ukrainian project" only to gain personal wealth and influence.

Of course, Ukraine also draws a certain picture of Soviet Russia. As was already stated before, the Ukrainian People's Republic is very important for contemporary Ukrainian history and politics. In fact, this period is a cornerstone of the Ukrainian state in an ideological sense. The Bolsheviks as enemies of the UPR are also introduced as the historical enemies of the Ukrainian state and national idea.

Ukrainian media emphasize the aggressive imperial politics of the Bolsheviks and their annexation of the territory of the UPR. The Battle of Kruty, Bazar, and other similar episodes are condemned as war crimes and portrayed as great sacrifices by the Ukrainian nation. The Bolsheviks who invaded Ukraine are depicted as bloodthirsty and barbaric. Ukrainian soldiers are heroes and defenders. Ukrainian culture suffers from ages-long oppression by the Russian Empire and its successors.

Top Soviet leaders are also depicted in a different light. Vladimir Lenin is a criminal and mass murderer who had goals that were far away from supporting and protecting the proletariat. Bolshevik military leaders are simply gangsters and rapists, etc.

Of course, in times of military conflict, all countries, even democratic and free ones, start a propaganda campaign — or will be quickly defeated. To a certain extent, there are light propagandistic messages in Ukrainian media. And, of course, it influences the perception of national history, especially such important periods as the UPR. In this way, rational analysis should be applied to the arguments and facts presented by both sides of the controversy.

In this respect, the situation of the UPR with propaganda is similar to the period of 2014–22. After understanding that there was no realistic diplomatic solution to the conflict with Soviet Russia, Ukrainian People's Republic officials began to mobilize the population of the country by using patriotic messages and building a professional army. Russian historians usually claim that this professional army was never built and that the UPR armed forces were weak even compared to such "ataman" gang leaders as Nestor Mahno. According to them, this was one of the main factors defining the UPR as just a puppet state, a "trick card" used in diplomacy by the real geopolitical players.

It is a slightly different military situation nowadays. The Ukrainian army, especially in the final period of the ATO/JFO, was quite experienced and strong. Russian propaganda, however, still stated that it was actually a mercenary gang that was remotely controlled by NATO. There were messages in the media stating that there were no ethnic Ukrainians in the army anymore, that most of the mercenaries came from Europe, and that they tended to be violent to the native Ukrainian population, which was yet another reason to "protect" it.

A separate and extremely important topic is the capitalism-versus-socialism controversy. In the UPR era, socialism and communism were completely new ideas for the mass population of the country. Western countries had a richer history of socialism—from the early ideas of French philosophers and the resulting revolution to Karl Marx and both his theoretical and political activity.

The Russian Empire was a closed society, where most of the population had no access to such ideas due to a lack of education. Of course, there were socialist activists and agitators—Lenin's organization as well as the October Revolution did not grow from a blank space. But most of the population were uneducated peasants who were denied the right of education by corrupt elites. It was the same situation on the territory of Ukraine.

This was probably one of the main reasons why communist propaganda was so extremely successful among the population of the rural areas of UPR. Peasants were promised what most of the revolts were started for—their own private land and freedom of agrarian entrepreneurship. Of course, this promise was eventually proven a lie. After closing the NEP and starting collectivization, farmers were put in a more dependent and oppressed state than in the preceding period. But at that time, the propaganda message of agitators was extremely successful.

Stalin's Soviet Union, of course, did not give any opportunities to articulate protest against such strict policy in the agrarian sector. Moreover, at a certain point, peasants were wiped out physically as a part of the program of industrialization. Purely economic factors in the Soviet Union were tightly connected to politics.

Nowadays, there is a very complex view of communism in Ukrainian society. It is understandable that neither Soviet communism nor developed socialism are the type of society of which French revolutionaries or Marx dreamt. People do not really believe the message about free land and decent salary for workers. Nevertheless, there are a lot of elderly citizens who are nostalgic for the society of the past.

This nostalgia is culturally defined. It refers more to the way of life, everyday culture, and the Zeitgeist of the epoch than to objective economic or political arguments. This nostalgia, however, is strong enough to influence the large social group and their choices during elections.

Most of the representatives of the younger generation embrace the capitalistic market and the opportunities it brings. Usually such a position is connected to also embracing Ukrainian nationalism and its supporting ideology. That is quite interesting from a sociological point of view. According to the classical communistic position, it is natural because nationalism and ultranationalism, as well as even fascism, are the products of capitalistic society.

There are, of course, younger people who deny the Ukrainian national idea. Their sympathy is usually for contemporary Russia and the Slavic world in general. Until 2022, they also influenced the sociology of the country, but the full-scale invasion changed the situation drastically. For better or for worse, there is no place for plurality of opinions in the state at war.

The opposing side of the debate is also influenced by culture. The negative picture of the Soviet Union is especially emphasized by the political repressions and planned economy. It is, again, the topic for many heated debates by professional and amateur historians.

To sum up—communism in contemporary Ukraine is viewed completely differently than in the UPR mostly due to historical reasons. Most of the pro-Russian people, especially among the young, tend to embrace the contemporary message about traditional values and the morally flawed West more than the image of the old Soviet society.

The ideological debates of the two periods of 1917–22 and 2014–22 have many formal differences, but their core remains the same—questions of identity and the resulting questions of morality. All the resulting historical debates from Mazepa to the Second World War are just forms of these two core issues. Propagandists from both sides know this fact and concentrate their efforts accordingly.

5. Major Shifts in Power

The events of the First World War and the February and October Revolutions brought major changes in the world's geopolitics and defined historical development for the coming century. Soviet Russia was a major political factor for both Asia and Europe, and later it had a complicated relationship with the United States of America. In the early period, these events concern policy on the territory of Ukraine as well. The emergence of the Ukrainian People's Republic would have been impossible without the mentioned historical dispositions.

Although the existence of the separate Ukrainian state in the beginning of the century was not a major factor for global politics, it had important consequences for the region of Eastern Europe. Some of the central events of the civil war in the former Russian Empire took place on this territory.

The factual circumstances of the emergence of the UPR are already described in the corresponding chapter. Nevertheless, it is useful to review them in light of more global events in the region of Eastern Europe as well as in a more non-political and non-military context. The birth and death of the young Ukrainian state, whatever Russian propaganda states, was an extremely important period both for Eastern Europe in the beginning of the 20th century and for the contemporary state of independent Ukraine.

The importance of the period can be understood from the complex attention that contemporary historians and political scientists give to this particular period. Just as was implied in the first chapter, if there is a most tragic and ideology-making moment in the history of Ukraine, it is (and is also for most of Europe) the moment of the Second World War and crimes against humanity committed on the territory of the country. Nevertheless, the undisputable second place for such a title goes to the First World War and the short existence of the Ukrainian People's Republic.

We look to the period of 1917–22 when we want to see the origins of our statehood as well as the roots of our geopolitical disposition on the world's map and our relations with neighboring countries. After all, you cannot understand the reasons and the consequences of the Second World War without at least a vague idea about the First World War and its consequences.

As for the contemporary epoch, it has a defining preceding historical event as well—the collapse of the Soviet Union. The role and the influence of this event for the period of 2014–22 was already emphasized in the previous chapters. The collapse of this giant geopolitical bloc can be compared to the diplomatic activity of the period after the First World War. Both events determined the form of international relations for the coming decades.

The Revolution of Dignity was also a very important event. It was not as global as the Soviet Union collapse, but it was a policy-forming event for the Ukrainian state as well as a definitive factor for eastern European diplomacy for the next few years. Russian officials considered the event to be in the same vein as the Western campaign of operations for political influence, and we could see the corresponding changes in Russian foreign policy during that period. The historical and cultural factors in the formation of the situation in contemporary Ukrainian, however, should be highlighted and the connection to the "rules of the game" of the previous political period should be shown.

So, what is the purpose of this particular chapter? What facts and processes concerning such shifts in power cannot be classified as either local policy and politics or world diplomacy? Actually, quite a few of such facts and processes, which encompass mostly the culture of the period, cannot be classified so.

The terms "globalism" and "globalization" were introduced much later than the emergence of the Ukrainian People's Republic. For sure, there were a lot of global processes, including socio-political relations of the different regions and imperialism, that introduced imperial policy of a completely new quality at that time. It was those global processes that defined the First World War, but no one thought about it in those terms yet. However, just as in the case of UPR-versus-Soviet Russia discourse, it could be called a major foreshadowing of what was to come in the future. That foreshadowing is worth analyzing.

The First World War was an event that brought not only political and diplomatic but also economic changes to the world. It was the first conflict of such a scale that was caused due to not only political reasons important for the ruling elites but also purely financial reasons. It was a starting point for the formation of the world's global corporate culture that brought the synthesis of politics and economy. It is due to these distant events that contemporary transnational corporations and their programs exist with their influence on the world.

Contemporary Russian propaganda often emphasizes the corporate organization of Western society, claiming that having economic reasons for political or even military actions is fundamentally immoral. Is that really the case? Probably yes. But are contemporary Russian politics completely free from rational decisions that are based on economic parameters? Of course not. And, of course, the same goes for Soviet Russia. After all, basing the political program on the economic situation is a cornerstone of Marxist ideology.

As for the contemporary epoch, the situation is much clearer. It is evident that many political events described in the previous chapters had their consequences for the world, including cultural, and vice versa. Eastern Europe's internal conflicts were defined by new global trends, and the result of these internal conflicts influenced some of those trends in return. The connection of the two periods in this context also should be studied.

The First World War was the trigger of the October Revolution and the end of the Russian Empire just as the collapse of the metropole Soviet Empire caused most of the next armed conflicts in the "colonies" because all those conflicts were the consequences of existing issues in Soviet society. The echo of the Soviet Union still resonates—it continues in contemporary frozen conflicts in South Ossetia, Abkhazia, the events that unfolded in Nagorno-Karabach, and old wounds in Chechnya and Transnistria. The military campaigns surrounding the few years of existence of the UPR were the product of the existing issues in the internal policy of the Russian Empire.

Take the role of Poland and the Polish war against Soviet Russia as well as the later annexation of the territory of Ukraine (which was its ally for a brief time), for example. It is evident that the imperial, or rather quasi-imperial, ambitions of Polish leaders were the echo of the spread of the national idea among the Poles during occupation by the Russian Empire in the 19th century. It involves both the national culture and such military campaigns as the Polish Rebellions in 1830–31 and in 1863–64.

Nation, nationality, and the set of problems surrounding these notions is still a very important issue in the contemporary world. The geopolitical context, however, is a little bit different. In the period of the UPR, a young and strong communist doctrine condemned all nation-oriented ideology as bourgeois brainwashing targeted at suppressing the political conscience of the proletarians. We cannot, of course, admit that as truth, at least not in such a radical way.

Contemporary Russia, as was mentioned earlier, relates to the communist past when it has a political meaning but holds a completely different official ideology. And Russian nationalism is the vital part of this ideology. Nowadays, Russian culture is proclaimed to be in opposition to Western culture in a way similar to the situation of the Cold War but with subtle and important differences.

It is precisely the moment when culture creates a political impact that leads both to the military campaigns and major changes in the policy after those events, the major shifts in power. And this is an important topic for profound study.

The exact causes of the First World War are still a field for discussions. It is mostly agreed that those causes deal with the rise of the new powerful players among the world's leading countries and the inevitable battle for resources of colonies and new markets in which to sell products of industry. In this way, this event is closely connected to the notion of imperialism in politics.

Imperialism is quite an interesting concept as it is. In today's world, no country would call itself an empire or strive to become one; imperialism is condemned as a morally and legally wrong doctrine. A leader of a country should at least proclaim officially that their goals are about prosperity and common good while respecting international law. In the early 20th century, the situation was a little bit different. Establishing imperial dominance in the world's military and economic sphere as well as political control over the group of colonies was the only way to economic prosperity and progress. And that was a logical continuation of nationalism, a radical understanding of the national idea and the propagation of national culture without international humanism.

The system of international law and relations was also in a very different form than it is today. International laws are violated even now (take the Russian invasion as an obvious example), but a country is at least required to propose a justification for its aggressive actions if its leaders don't want to be isolated.

In the early 20th century, the international community was very young, and nationalism was influencing the world's stage to a far greater extent. To become an aggressive militarized imperial or quasi-imperial state seemed the shortest way to prosperity and the common good of the citizens of the country. It was "automatically" morally justified among the population.

More to that—many citizens demanded the military action of the country and considered such demands as patriotism and propagating national culture. The Springtime of Nations happened in Europe in 1848, and the idea of nationalism in many places only then began to develop. The status of "nationalism" as an ideology in the contemporary world also differs from that of the beginning of the 20th century.

Nationalism and imperialism were the targets of criticism for the communists and especially Vladimir Lenin. Russian Bolsheviks claimed that the First World War was the "imperial war," an inevitable catastrophe caused by following false ideological doctrine. Lenin condemned imperialism as the last stage of development of capitalistic society.

Of course, contemporary criticism of imperialism does not involve the same socialist theses. After all, the state created by Lenin and his followers was one of the greatest and most aggressive empires in human history. It is useful to outline such criticism, however, as it is another interesting detail of the ideological debates surrounding the main problems of this book.

What is the contemporary criticism of imperialism and imperial ideology then? It was already mentioned that colonization and the military aggression it involves are condemned as antidemocratic in modern society, but what is the cornerstone of that criticism? Are democracy and the need to reach the status of a recognized democratic structure the only reasons we consider imperialism a wrong doctrine today?

In one of the previous paragraphs concerning the problem, the moral side of the question was mentioned. Morality is the natural foundation of political philosophy, but it is doubtful that "imperial" players of the beginning of the century viewed it that way. Imperialism as the doctrine of domination dismisses morality, or at least puts it in second place after the prosperity that dominance brings.

It should be stated that the unique situation when international law, human rights, and the morality of politics begins to play a role in assessing that politics was made possible only in the middle of the 20th century, after the Second World War. The horrors of WWII made humanity review its values in the context of the danger of complete extinction. The First World War and the rise of the aggressive militarized ideologies was only the stage preceding the next Great War. Nevertheless, if a new global conflict begins, we will have to admit that all those sacrifices had only cosmetic effects for global policy.

Another sign of this pivotal moment in the world's history is the first attempt to codify and justify such concepts as "human rights." Human rights belong to every human being as the basic human dignity by the right of birth as a representative of humankind. These rights include such notions as safety, freedom of thought, and protection of the law. Of course, none of the human rights are compatible with the fascism, totalitarian communism, or imperialism.

Unfortunately, human rights became both the tool and an object of speculation for the geopolitical struggles of the Cold War era. No matter how you particularly assess the political situation in the world and the role of human rights in those struggles, you should admit that status as a "tool" diminishes the importance of the concept as a fundamental cornerstone of humanism.

Nevertheless, it took approximately 30 years of political development for the society of the First World War to admit to the concept of human rights. It just needs to be said that the path to this fundamental concept started right at this point, at the triumph of imperialism and different other aggressive militaristic political programs. The same can be stated about the system of global international security and international law.

It can be surmised that there is a particular ideological source for all those ideas, like democracy and human rights. It was mentioned in the preceding discussion. It is humanism. The ideal of respect and empathy for human dignity and freedom of the individual. Throughout history, humanism was always sort of the "underground" idea. It developed in the works of artists and scholars in a hidden form, emerging in the official political discourse only in the 20th century.

Humanism as an idea and the element of progress in human society is often studied by different works in the humanities. It does not mean, unfortunately, that humanism won in this particular period of history. There are numerous details in recent events that prove that a lot of people on the globe do not take that idea seriously — these events include wars, economic crises, and crime.

But it should be emphasized that it is only recently that the idea of humanism was introduced into official discourse. You did not need to justify war with another country in the Middle Ages — there was not an idea that other people had any rights or that a principle of freedom should not be violated. The wars were started as part of the standard life cycle, and simple citizens were just passive spectators of everyday terrors. And the introduction of that doctrine started with the tragic aftermath of the Great War.

The Ukrainian People's Republic and its history are tightly connected to the First World War as well. It would never have come into existence in the first place without the collapse and crisis of political authority in the Russian Empire caused by the First World War. And the end of the UPR was not only due to the issues of internal policy and military events, but also because there was no place for this young state in the minds of the diplomatic elite of Europe and the USA at that time.

Why there was no such place is an interesting question for the special "diplomatic" chapter, but the general culture and global processes in the background of these events and decisions is a question for this particular one. There is a connection between the culture and diplomacy too, of course.

Were we to search for the cultural reason of that diplomatic "failure" of the UPR, we would find that it lies in history, including the Springtime of Nations of the 19th century. The territory of Ukraine was under the Russian Empire's rule and the "spring" did not happen, but European revolutions had major consequences for Ukraine. These consequences were the start of Ukrainian political self-awareness, which through complex cultural and sociopolitical development led to the emergence of the UPR and, later, through that stage, to the contemporary state of Ukraine.

Nevertheless, there was an important detail—all those events happened much later than for other European countries gaining their national independence and separate political cultures. The Ukrainian People's Republic was just not part of that process. During the Paris Peace Conference, Ukraine as a separate country was a very young concept. People just did not know enough about the Ukrainian nation as a separate culture that requires political independence.

Is the situation different in contemporary discourse? Ukraine is still poorly represented in the global cultural context, although it gained official political independence from the Soviet Union. The culture of the nation, the culture of the country, and its popularity around the world have direct political and diplomatic impact on the events occurring in the region.

Russian propaganda will, of course, say something completely different about that situation, including the period of the UPR. The "Springtime of Nations" was an event connected to the development of nationalism as doctrine and was actually a stage of development of European imperialism. And Ukraine was just a tool of expansion for those militaristic forces in European society. This is all consistent with the "Bismarck's Plan" idea.

Russian discourse emphasizes the unfolding of the UPR as the vital event for an understanding of the history of the region. According to it, the UPR was used by the Western elites, deprived of material resources, and then betrayed in the political and military sense. And the only purpose of its existence was to destabilize Russia, first the Russian Empire and then a new Soviet Russia. The UPR was a child of European imperial politics, and its short history was a tragedy of tyranny and moral corruption that would be recreated during the Second World War in a much bloodier form.

As for the contemporary situation, the picture is even more catastrophic. The collapse of the Soviet Union was a major tragic event, and countries that gained independence due to that event are actually moral wrongdoers and traitors. Ukraine is considered one of the main traitors, thereby admitting its cultural relations to European society. Contemporary Russian propaganda draws an ancestral tree for European culture with its roots in the imperial politics of Nazi Germany.

That is, of course, an evident misinterpretation of the situation, especially from the point of view of the average Ukrainian. But propaganda works by its own laws, and the myth about descendance and morality in the minds of people is much more important than the objective situation and the subtleties of the cultural differences between nations and historical periods. That is, again, a question about the political and media culture of contemporary Russian society.

A critic might comment that actually today's Russian society is a descendant of the Soviet Empire, which was militaristic and morally nihilistic in the same way as Nazi Germany. The differences and similarities between the two periods were discussed in one of the previous chapters. As was already outlined, however, contemporary Russian ideology, despite the numerous differences from the socialist view on things, gladly admits its role as a descendant of that state.

What is more, the Soviet state and its legacy is one of the ideological cornerstones for Putin's Russia. There are many reasons why the situation is like that, but most lie in the events of the Second World War and the "greatest political myth" connected to it in the minds of the citizens of the Russian Federation. In this context, the events of the preceding periods are just supportive facts and discourses for the main "picture."

The First World War is often called the real beginning of the 20th century and the catastrophic events that occurred in global politics of this period. Russian historian Peter Struve made a famous claim that any war and even political event after the Great War will be just its continuation. This is indeed true about most of the world's diplomacy, politics, and global economic processes that happened before the next big war. It is also evident that, in a way, the great event of the Second World War was caused by the unsolved diplomatic and political issues left after the First World War.

In a sense, we can call WWII the delayed continuation of the great clashes of WWI. Geopolitical players did not reach their goals and did not satisfy their main interests such that the next great conflict was absolutely inevitable. The same "continuation concept" can be applied to the Cold War, the moral and political problems surrounding the invention of nuclear weapons, a possible Third World War, as well as the numerous contemporary regional conflicts.

There were several guiding ideas about the Great War that continued on in European society after it ended. Some of them (e.g., imperialism) were already outlined, and they all can be summed up as the details of a new global culture that began to be dominant in the world in the 20th century. The struggle between these ideas of dominance and oppression and the ideas of humanism and freedom became the main "motive" of the modern world.

The First World War was an historical event that influenced not only the military and diplomatic history of the world, but also the fabric of the social relations in the global human community. It was the first time in history when mass propaganda was used to form the opinion of the population and mobilize it for a major war effort. It was the beginning of the work of secret services and affiliated diplomacy as well as counterintelligence in forms close to the contemporary world. It was also the first conflict when mechanization and the mass production of heavy industry were such important factors. The importance of the economic reasons for the conflict as well as the birth of corporate culture was already outlined.

The First World War also marks an important stage for the development of military psychiatry. The condition now known as PTSD (post-traumatic stress disorder) was called "shell shock" then and was connected by researchers mostly to the active usage of artillery. Of course, soldiers endured heavy psychological traumas in the wars of the past as well, but it was precisely this conflict when it became such a mass event and such a big problem for postwar society. It also may be said that the psychological aftermath of those events had such a huge impact on society that we can talk about the collective psychological trauma just as in the case of a famine or pandemic.

PTSD and connected problems also mark the extent to which the global conflict was dehumanizing society. With mass industrial production and a mass war effort, mental health, which previously was the field for few chosen specialists, also became a global social problem. A new approach to these problems was invented, and however debatable the effectiveness of the new psychiatric system was, it evidently would have its negative, dehumanizing impact on human society.

Military inventions were also a major factor, although we can read about them in a lot more sources than we can about the new factors in social life. It was the first major mobilization on such a scale of the population both for industrial purposes and as conscripts for the army. It was the first usage of poisonous gas as a weapon—a weapon of mass destruction. The weaponization of poisonous gas can be compared to the invention of the nuclear bomb at the end of the Second World War. Both were massive tragedies and raised a lot of moral and ethical questions concerning using knowledge and technology for war in the context of humanism and common sense. It introduced military aviation on a scale that really influences combat. It was the first usage of tanks and of a completely new role for artillery strikes.

After the events of the Great War, the world's diplomacy had a major change. Leading experts understood that if such conflicts cannot be prevented in the future, the human race is doomed to extinction. This was understood long before the Second War and the creation of nuclear weapons, but it became an even more important problem during the events of the Cold War.

The international organization of the League of Nations was formed with main functions to support global international security and prevent conflicts. As we all know now, this organization was ineffective and could not cope with its main goal—preventing the Second World War. After the devastating conflict, the League of Nations was dissolved, and the United Nations (UN) was formed instead.

There is, however, a lot of criticism concerning the UN today, especially in light of the war in Ukraine, which is the most devastating conflict in Europe since the World Wars. The United Nations did not prevent this conflict. Debaters from the Ukrainian side blame the organization for the lack of support and light international pressure on Russia. For their part, Russians claim that Ukraine is a fascist state, and their military operation is merely securing the borders and the Russian-speaking population of Donbass and other regions. Russian propaganda marks the importance of the moral justification of political action in the contemporary world again, and this topic becomes another hot battlefield for propaganda.

Another important series events for our understanding of the role of the United Nations in the contemporary conflict and the preceding Donbass War are the Balkan Wars of the 1990s. This series of conflicts happened between different ethnic and political groups on the territory of the former Yugoslavia. In a sense, it was another consequence of the collapse of the Soviet Union and the change in the global political system. The governmental political structure that held the society of the state ceased to be, and the hidden internal conflicts in that society gave birth to horrible acts of violence.

At a certain point, the United Nations and the international community decided to intervene. It is debatable whether that intervention prevented or created more violence. The UN was blamed again for taking sides in the conflicts and for supporting certain factions and trying to mitigate the influence of others. The enemies of the peacekeepers claimed that it is immoral to claim that you are trying to resolve the conflict while still searching for the political benefits from it.

The Balkan Wars of the 1990s are still a very debatable topic in Russia and its affiliated world. Many volunteers from other Slavic countries went to the former Yugoslavia to fight mostly against the Western World (or so they thought). There is strong moral condemnation of the peacekeeping force in this conflict among the representatives of contemporary Russian society.

Was the peacekeeping initiative in this conflict a failure? It is hard to tell. Due to the political consequences, the United Nations had to review its policy concerning similar future conflicts. The position of the international community during 2014 and even 2022 is shaped by the experience of the Balkan Wars in the 1990s.

Meanwhile, the Russian Federation uses Balkan Wars to boost its own ideological agenda in Eastern Europe and beyond. In Russian words, Ukraine is a state where destructive, ultranational, radical forces came to power such that it is dangerous to the world's community. In this way, they justify both the support of the separatists during the ATO/JFO and the full-scale invasions of 2022. Of course, the UN cannot take sides in the conflict. This is not only due to the reasons described in the previous paragraph, but also because while condemning the invasion, it should follow its own rules and procedures. This ambiguity makes the political debates around the problem even hotter. There are different factions inside the world's diplomatic society as well. Not everyone is voting for Ukraine or against Russia.

These are all contemporary debates, but they have their roots in history and especially in the period of the Ukrainian People's Republic. In the previous chapter, it was mentioned and argued several times and is the main idea here that the same relations influence the global events and processes that defined the UPR and today's Ukraine.

There was definitely an international community at that time, especially in Europe. It is just that it did not proclaim the same values as the contemporary community in Europe. In fact, the disposition was more weighted toward imperial politics. We can say that such a disposition was dooming the continent to a devastating war in the future, as happened with the First World War.

Is the moral position so tightly connected to the military and political events? After all, the critic might say that the contemporary world and the UN are no better and that the international community just proclaims that it follows certain moral and political obligations while giving birth to the new conflicts.

That is actually consistent with Russian propaganda, according to which the UN is an artificial structure fully controlled by the United States of America. In fact, its only function is justifying the global politics of neocolonialism. Russian propaganda usually bases its claims on the political myth of the Second World War and emphasizing that it was the international community that allowed for the development of fascist and Nazi ideology in the heart of Europe.

It seems like a giant complex conspiracy theory. It was, however, a Nazi propagandist who proved that such eclectic and eccentric concepts actually work quite well with brainwashed and indoctrinated people. There is only one rational way out of this ideological dilemma—rational doubt toward both official doctrines. Being skeptical about the official discourse of Western society does not mean that we should immediately turn to another political mythology.

Russian propaganda is mythological. It establishes certain historical and cultural events, like the thoroughly mentioned Second World War and contemporary politics toward LGBTQ rights, and makes them sacred objects. It can seem irrational and an odd strategy, but it works. To gain a deeper understanding of those myths, we should again turn to the shifts in power during the establishment of the Soviet regime.

The October Revolution was, in a sense, a bigger shift in Russian society than the Great War. The old social hierarchy and the political foundation of the state were completely broken. Bolsheviks brought a completely new system inspired by socialist theories and the events of the French Revolution. It had a profound philosophy behind it based on the works of some of the most advanced scholars and humanists in the history of humankind. The resulting state, however, turned out to be one of the most oppressive and tyrannical societies in the world.

The new socialist society was alien to the people who had been born in the times of the Russian Empire. How the economy and political life were organized was a strange and novel way to rule the society. Researchers sometimes talk about an absolutely different type of civilization, Soviet civilization, but it proved to be extremely effective, especially in terms of political and ideological control. The new Soviet society and Soviet way of thinking quickly assimilated most of the population of the former Russian Empire.

Political persecutions, the new politics in law enforcement, and the growing role of the political police played their role in shaping the new society. In addition to the genetic collective psychological trauma caused by mass hunger, another similar trauma was caused by the political persecution campaigns of the 1930s. Millions of people were persecuted, and almost every citizen in the country lived in constant terror of arrest.

The elimination of potential enemies that was conducted by Stalin and his followers served both purely political and ideological purposes. From the point of view of economy and even simple common sense, those actions were completely irrational, but it seems that Bolsheviks had their special ideal of society and followed it. The public security of the country was indeed very advanced such that it was almost impossible for the spy or rebel to exist within Soviet society.

But it was not only about political persecutions. Global changes in social and economic life also occurred. One of the previous chapters already spoke of the new economic system and its influence on the political life of the country and the newly annexed territories. The social life of a citizen was controlled from birth to death. For most of the citizens, their complete life span was planned by the government down to the tiny details. All the non-professional organizations were controlled by authorities, and the education system was an object of politically motivated shaping and reshaping as well.

But what is interesting here is not the mature Soviet society as it was (it was already discussed), but the particular shift that made the October Revolution and all the following events possible. In the previous paragraphs, the imperialism and the militarism of Europe and the consequences for the First World War as well as the development of nationalism were outlined. Communist society, however, officially condemns all those ideas and concepts as morally flawed and positions itself in strong political opposition toward them. Does that mean socialism, including Lenin's variant, is the "rational pole" of geopolitics?

We have already argued that, actually, it does not. Lenin's state was aggressive and militaristic. The changes to the economy indeed brought major shifts in social life, but they were not what social utopists and theoreticians foresaw. We could also turn to the experience of contemporary Russia, which often relates to the Soviet past but is, in fact, based more on the foundations of nationalism and even savage imperialism.

The interesting question here is actually why this is so. Why did Vladimir Lenin fail at creating a utopia and create an aggressive empire instead? Bolsheviks and their cruel methods are well known by historians, and any attempt to reintroduce them as actual social utopists are doomed to be part of the virulent propaganda. But we could still say, in the same vein as some of the famous quotes by Lenin himself, that methods actually do not matter; what matters is the political aim, the result of your political actions.

The Bolsheviks fulfilled their political program within the borders of the Russian Empire. The capitalistic social institutions were ruined, and the completely new system of relations was established. But the fact remains—the new society was far from the utopia described by Marx and other socialists. Does that mean that socialist ideology does not work in reality?

Socialism and Marxism were tremendously influential ideas in the first part of the 20th century. They shaped politics and international relations, including provoking revolutions and wars. But it seems that, in the end, methods do matter. Bolsheviks committed awful crimes during the Civil War, and those crimes influenced the political outcome of the whole campaign, for sure.

One of the early chapters described how the corrupt Russian Empire gained more and more internal social pressure and how the Bolsheviks used that internal conflict at the critical moment, but it was only a sociological view of things. Did the Russian Revolution bring relief? Not for the simple citizens. Marxism is still an important doctrine and communism a very influential ideology, but in the light of the historical context discussed, we cannot consider it the panacea anymore.

It seems that we can sum up by saying that the culture that includes methods used to pursue political aims is actually prior to the social, political, and economic structures. It is the only way we can explain the many paradoxes of the major shifts in power of the 20th century that made the First World War and the subsequent events possible.

6. Diplomacy and International Relations

The diplomatic disposition surrounding both the existence of the UPR and the contemporary situation in Ukraine was mentioned several times in the previous chapters. A detailed analysis, however, was not conducted, although it is both interesting and extremely important for our understanding of the political and strategic implications. This chapter conducts that analysis.

The Ukrainian People's Republic was situated in a very complex net of international relations mostly at the intersection of the interests of European countries and the newly formed Soviet Russia. As was mentioned before, a lot of Ukrainian politics is defined by its geographical location as the "bridge" between West and East. Soviet Russia is an obvious eastern influence, whereas western influences are connected mostly to Europe.

As for contemporary Ukraine, much in the above paragraph remains true. Ukraine is still suffering a global identity crisis concerning its position between eastern and western culture. Different geographical regions of the country were formerly parts of different countries with separate histories and cultures, and it creates complex culture specifics for each reason. However enriching it is as phenomena, it makes it difficult to create a unified society based on the national idea.

Global players often use these cultural specifics to establish diplomatic contacts with Ukraine. The western world traditionally works with the western and central regions of the country, which are more influenced by Europe, and Russia has a major support in the Donbass region as well as the southern regions of Ukraine. In one of the previous chapters, this regional division of the country was described as one of the prime factors for the politics inside the country, but it bears a great significance for international relations as well.

Different global blocs are associated with the different regions and different social groups inside the country. Local politicians, even of a high rank, can afford not to take that into consideration, but the diplomat of any level and any person whose political activity is connected to international relations should take this fact into consideration as vital. The same is true about any contemporary culture studies about Ukraine.

Before the First World War, the United States of America was quite a powerful country, but it was not the contemporary geopolitical giant until the end of the Second World War and the establishment of the new world order. In contemporary discourse, the main power in the Western World is the USA, but during the UPR period, it was Europe that mattered. Nevertheless, American diplomacy was an extremely important factor for the establishment of the post-war world order.

In today's world, Europe is still important due to its geographical position in relation to Ukraine. One of the main proclaimed goals of the Ukrainian government after the era of Yanukovich has been joining the European Union and the NATO military bloc. Russian opinion of the EU and Ukrainian attempts to join it was already outlined. NATO is a connected but separate problem that is very important for our understanding of the diplomatic side of the problem.

NATO is a military organization that was established in Europe after the Second World War to support peace and order. It quickly became one of the main antagonists of the Soviet Union and a competitor for this country's influence on the continent. It was also one of the main targets for Soviet and later Russian propaganda.

This propaganda usually refers to the set of agreements that were reached between the West and the newly established Russian government after the collapse of the Soviet Union. One agreement was the promise not to widen NATO's influence in Eastern Europe because it would be a direct attack on Russia's strategic interests in the region and security. Ukrainian officials usually claim that this agreement was broken by Russians themselves when they started covert intelligence and military operations against Ukraine.

The idea of Ukraine joining NATO and the EU is not a new one, however. Pro-western and pro-nationalist political parties inside Ukrainian society advocated these ideas for years and reached a sort of a peak of the debates in 2004 during and shortly after the Orange Revolution. Pro-Russian members of Ukrainian society usually met those attempts to advocate such an agenda with political protests. In the eyes of those citizens, joining NATO is joining the aggressive military bloc, something equal to siding with the fascists in the Second World War.

This geopolitical choice is also closely correlated with the classical political Ukrainian "dichotomies," such as the question of the official language. Supporting NATO is closely associated with the nationalist policy and establishing the Ukrainian language as the only official language in the country. This is but another detail that shows how close the connection between the purely diplomatic issues and the internal political issues of Ukraine is.

During the period preceding the First World War, the western part of Ukraine, as was outlined before, was under the political administration of the Austro-Hungarian Empire. This period had its impact on culture and deepened the cultural differences between the inhabitants of the different regions of Ukraine. We have to deal with some of the consequences of this process even today. In times of war, an especially tragic event took place whenever fellow Ukrainians had to fight each other because they were drafted to the armies on both sides of the frontline.

What is important for diplomacy is that the western regions of Ukraine were perceived in central Europe as a province of the Austro-Hungarian Empire, which resulted in a final decision to admit them to be part of the legacy of that state. It resulted in support of Poland instead of Ukraine. Some historians usually refer to the fate of the Western Ukrainian People's Republic as a great betrayal of both the international community and its allies from the central regions of the UPR.

Europe was also transforming at that time. The Austro-Hungarian Empire was ruined both politically and economically, and Germany was in very bad economic shape as well. It was evident that great political changes awaited these countries. These were two big players in Europe who tried to gamble everything in a game against the British Empire, which was still the main colonial empire on the globe at that time. They lost the First World

War, but due to many reasons and events, Great Britain also lost its imperial status. The power centers started to shift to the United States of America. The USA fixed its place as the new world's main superpower at the end of WWII and became the world's only superpower after the collapse of the Soviet Union.

Nevertheless, in the interwar period, the world's political balance was still in the process of formation. In this way, the main center of decision-making about the world's new geopolitical model was rather situated in France. The central post-war diplomatic event, the Paris Peace Conference, happened in the capital of that country. This conference included the UPR's delegation and was extremely important for the Republic's political future.

The UPR delegation's mission at the Paris Peace Conference, however, ended as a failure. They could not persuade Europe to continue to support the Ukrainian People's Republic. Although a certain amount of support was given, the final "vote" was for Poland and other neighboring countries' territorial ambitions. There were several reasons for such an outcome.

Ukraine was in the sphere of interest of Germany and the Austro-Hungarian Empire, at least in the starting stages of the Great War. This region was key for weakening and defeating the Russian Empire on the Eastern Front. Germans indeed conducted military intelligence operations and gave a lot of attention to the local culture (though "Bismarck's Plan" is obvious propaganda). The historical chapter has outlined how the Skoropadsky government was established with the support of the German military.

Were German political actions in the region a success or a failure? Germans had managed to retake the military initiative from the Russian Empire and influence the political disruptions in Russian society. Nevertheless, Soviet Russia eventually regained all the lost territories and political power. What was part of the political manipulation to weaken the tsarist Russian Empire grew to become a very important factor in the European political arena. Soviet Russia later became a powerful opponent and competitor of the central European countries and especially Germany. There is a certain irony here.

The history of the relations between the Ukrainian People's Republic and Germany was an important factor that defined the future of the UPR. "Old Europe" saw the UPR as a puppet state that did not represent the independent culture and the independent nation. What is more, it was an ally of the Central Powers. This was the primary reason why Great Britain, France, and other big players did not support the Ukrainian delegation at the Paris Peace Conference.

Neighboring countries had their own territorial ambitions concerning the Ukrainian lands. The situation of the "triangle of death" that mostly caused the military defeat of the Ukrainian People's Republic forces was already mentioned. These territorial ambitions also made the neighbors support the anti-Ukrainian diplomatic position, including at the Paris Peace Conference.

That was, of course, a major violation of international law and a predatory morality. The position could be called imperialistic in its nature. It contradicted the diplomatic rules and procedures established by the main international players themselves, but it was required by the political agenda. Once more in history, practical politics won over moral principles.

Russian propaganda usually claims that this situation shows how immoral Western society is for following a completely practical agenda without giving any attention to the morality of the situation and such humanitarian problems as the existence of the independent Ukrainian nation and culture. In the times of the UPR, the debate was additionally sharpened by communist political ideology. Russian communists saw Europe and the Triple Entente as imperialist aggressors who had caused the previous conflict and were fundamentally morally corrupt. Communists claimed that this decision as well as all the other unfair politics of those "players" are products of the capitalistic society and its lack of moral foundations.

In this way, the world's communist revolution was seen as a moral struggle, the fight of the righteous forces against the darkest bourgeois reaction. It is still a powerful ideological concept, and during the UPR era, when socialism was much younger and there was no extensive data on its possible social and moral failures, this ideology was extremely strong. Later, Lenin and Stalin would prove that they were ready for even more immoral decisions, especially when it concerned political power.

What is the diplomatic situation for Ukraine in the period of 2014–22? First of all, it should be emphasized that there is no sphere of social life that was as profoundly influenced and changed by the events of February 2022 as diplomacy. Ukraine was officially supported by the international community and the United Nations, and Russian aggression was officially condemned. Ukraine received a vast amount of direct technological, military, and financial support. The war also placed Ukraine, at least in the first months of the conflict, at the center of attention of the international community. There are certain political analysts who claim that after a year of war, the diplomatic community is growing tired of the "Ukrainian problem" and will probably cut support in the future, especially given the new conflict in Israel. Nevertheless, a fact is a fact—in the early stages of the conflict, Ukraine, as a country, received enormous international support.

In the times of the ATO/JFO, the situation was quite different. The separatists in the Donetsk and Luhansk regions were obviously supported by the Russian military forces and guided by their military commanders. The Russian position, however, was that ATO/JFO was actually a sort of civil war, a conflict inside Ukrainian society caused by unresolved conflicts, among which language and culture issues were foremost. And there were experts and opinion leaders in the West who supported that claim. This is the same as in the 1940s–50s, when some European intellectuals supported Stalin due to his achievements in fighting Nazism and out of general sympathy for the left-wing ideas despite the information about his horrible crimes committed inside the USSR.

This created a diplomatic situation around ATO/JFO when official representatives of Europe and the USA supported the sovereignty and territorial unity of Ukraine, but their main proclaimed aim was peace in the region, mostly through negotiations. Minsk-format negotiations were a failure for the Ukrainian government. The ceasefire was broken, and no progress for the reintegration of the lost territories was made. Separatists, for their part, also considered these negotiations to be a trickery of the West and a diplomatic failure because the ceasefire was broken (by Ukraine, they claim). Their political aims were at least autonomy inside the Ukrainian state, the widening of the political influence of the pro-Russian forces in the Ukrainian government, and the solving of the language question once and for all by establishing Russian as the second official language of the country. And some of the separatists dreamed of joining the Russian Federation, which would have been a complicated diplomatic event in the period preceding February 2022.

Western support during this period was also limited to non-lethal weapons and certain technical equipment. It sparked major discussions inside Ukrainian society because the lack of weapons was considered one of the main reasons why the separatist forces could not be defeated. Pro-Ukrainian debaters emphasized that the LPR and DPR received full military support from the Russian Federation, including elite troops and intelligence. Nevertheless, Western diplomacy did not want to worsen relations with Russia, and their military support for the separatists was hard to prove. In this situation, supporting the status quo seemed to be the most practical policy.

Besides, the Russian Federation was quite proficient in its diplomatic effort to blur the "lines" in the Donbass conflict. Propagandists inside the country portrayed the people of Donbass as oppressed and even victims of genocide by the Ukrainian army. In the international media, the Russian campaign represented Ukraine as an aggressive, militarized, and corrupt government, a classical fascist state struggling with freedom fighters who became rebels out of objective economic and cultural reasons. The internal propaganda was extremely effective at producing the needed opinions inside Russian society too. Throughout the years of Putin's rule in the country, the population was indoctrinated with profoundly negative opinions about the Ukrainian government and nation, which fostered the rapid growth of aggression and intolerance. The seeds of the future full-scale war were sown at that time.

Was the diplomatic disposition of the world's leading countries toward Ukraine in 2014–22 better than that of their counterparts toward the Ukrainian People's Republic in 1917–22? It is hard to say. From one point of view, Ukraine as an independent state is a far-more-known concept in the contemporary era than it was after the First World War. But this is due to globalization and the development of media (including the Internet) and not the cultural and diplomatic efforts of the Ukrainian government, unfortunately.

There is also no comparable negative context to Ukraine siding with a faction like the Central Powers, who were the enemies of the Entente. Nevertheless, there is another concept that is strongly propagated by the contemporary anti-Ukrainian media— connections with Nazi ideology. There is no such notion in the modern world as a "Nazi global political bloc" (despite the claims of Russian propaganda conspiracy theories), but there are powers (mostly underground and marginal) that support the ultra-right ideas. And it is enough to connect an entity to these powers to create an extremely negative ideological context.

In one of the previous chapters, the problem of radicals taking part in the Donbass conflict on both sides was already discussed. Of course, Nazis on the frontline are bad for public relations, but this is a minor problem compared to the political program of the government and the general ideology that is dominant in the society of that country.

Are modern Ukrainian politics ultra-right oriented? Even taking into consideration problems that are connected with the "language question" and all the culture-related issues, it is hard to call the Ukrainian society supportive of Nazi ideology. Another problem is that, as was mentioned before, the war in Donbass and the invasion of 2022 radicalized Ukrainian society more than any of the previous efforts of the nationalists inside the Ukrainian government.

But if we view only the period of 2014–22, we may say that the answer to the initial question is negative. Ukraine was not following either Nazi ideology or ultra-right ideology in general. Maybe it is nationalist-oriented, especially in the times of Poroshenko, but it is an evident fact that radical ultra-right wing forces in Ukrainian society were deep underground until the events of 2014. What is more, those events were mostly caused by Russia, which created a certain "sociological loop."

It can be summed up that during the Donbass conflict, the diplomatic situation around Ukraine was partially similar to the early years of the Ukrainian People's Republic. But it is only a partial similarity. In general, the cultural diplomacy in contemporary Ukraine is far better than it was from 1917 to 1922. There are, however, complex problems, especially those connected to the Russian propaganda and the political context of supporting right-wing ideas. Of course, the situation changes drastically after the Russian invasion of 2022 and is still developing (that is the prime reason why the preceding period is chosen for analysis).

To understand the connection of the two time periods better, we need to return to the history of the UPR and view the general picture of international relations in Europe in that era. The most important document here is probably the famous speech by US President Woodrow Wilson to the Congress on January 8, 1918, known as the "Fourteen Points." This was a defining document not only for US foreign policy but also for the Paris Peace Conference.

US diplomats played a large part in the Paris Peace Conference, and although the USA was not as influential as it would be after the Second World War, we can trace the general consensus of the event by the mentioned "Fourteen Points." Other countries were mostly in alignment with this document. Top-level US diplomats were working on the project of post-war Europe together with their European colleagues with Wilson's "points" in mind.

The most important point of the program is probably that which is about open diplomacy. Wilson proposed an end to the secret treaties and alliances and making all the big diplomatic agreements available to the public. This point is very humanist in nature, but an experienced diplomat would say it is impossible even in today's world. Many important agreements are still conducted secretly and are even semi-formal. In the interwar period, the diplomatic situation was even more complicated.

As we all know now, this point of Wilson's program was broken many times. Perhaps the most vivid example of exception to this rule is the Molotov-Ribbentrop Pact between Nazi Germany and the Soviet Union. Though the pact itself was public, there were secret parts of the document, and in general, this document was violating numerous norms of international law, human morality, and even the ideological dogmas of both participants.

There is, however, another example closer to the studied time period, namely the fate of Ukrainian lands and sovereignty after the Treaty of Riga, signed on March 18, 1921, that divided the UPR's territory between the newly formed independent Poland and the Soviet Union. The moral and geopolitical side of this problem was mentioned in the previous chapters. The Ukrainian People's Republic was betrayed by a former ally, but there is also a complicated international relations side of the problem here.

The Polish-Soviet War continued during the Paris Peace Conference, and, of course, the resulting treaty was majorly influenced by the general agreements reached by diplomatic elites of Europe and the USA at this event. Poland gained the geopolitical support and the agreements with the Soviet Union needed to make their annexation of part of Ukraine legal.

Of course, the Soviet Union was perceived as a major threat by European politicians, but it exerted its military might and the extensive political influence of the communist ideas all around the world. The Soviets managed to reach a political balance.

Now, was the Treaty of Riga absolutely normal from the point of view of "public diplomacy"? The official documents were available to the public and the annexation of the UPR's territory was impossible to hide. But was the support of Poland from the European diplomatic elite in this conflict a specifically moral decision? Was it not in violation of the spirit of the principles declared by Wilson earlier?

By now we know that this and other questionable diplomatic decisions resulted in another world war. The Treaty of Riga was signed, thereby not only breaking moral obligation and humanitarian considerations, but also perpetuating the diplomacy of the "closed elite." The interests of the population, their identity, and their opinions about politics were left out of view.

Those interests were sacrificed to reach a diplomatic consensus and establish relative stability in the region. One might say that peace is paramount even to the humanitarian consideration, but the question of the practical result of this decision inevitably follows. We have already established that the Second World War was the consequence of unresolved issues, the important part of which were international relations.

Wilson's "freedom of the seas" point is important for the general history but irrelevant in the given context. It can be introduced as part of the beginning of the process of globalization. This issue was discussed earlier already. The same goes for the point about the removal of economic barriers. After the First World War, the globe began to establish more and closer economic ties, which brought completely new consequences for international relations.

Wilson's point regarding the reduction of armament was very important, though. The arms race was a pivotal topic between the two World Wars and during the Cold War. This race not only consumed resources and radicalized the society, but also provoked the war. In the beginning of the 20th century and before the First World War, the world experienced its first such arms race (at least on such a global scale).

Stopping or slowing down the arms race has become a major humanitarian project and one of the primary problems for international relations, especially during the Cold War. There were positive changes after the collapse of the Soviet Union, when many countries cut their military budgets and weapons arsenals, including nuclear weapons. Unfortunately, the world of today is on the verge of a new arms race.

The arms race is evident in the period after February 2022. Member countries of the NATO military bloc supply Ukraine with weapons as well as non-lethal technical aid, and Russia and its allies are engaged in similar activity on the other side of the frontline. These supplies became one of the main topics in Ukrainian media coverage. The main factor in the world's military economics, however, is connected to China, its plans to support Russia, and to what limit.

Between 2014 and 2022, the situation was quite different. There was no positioning of Russia as a player who would try to use a full-scale war to regain imperial status. Most of the international community considered Russian support of the separatists in Ukraine as part of their strategy to uphold the government interests in Eastern Europe that should have been countered to a certain extent, but all in all, it was just another regional proxy conflict. The invasion of 2022 raised the stakes.

Nevertheless, most of the attention of the world community is given to China. Russia is seen as a proxy that influences Eastern Europe, and to a certain extent Central Asia, mostly according to the plan agreed with the Chinese government. Ukraine is an important indicator of what is happening on the world's stage, but it is secondary to the economic and political decisions of Beijing.

China is also the only country in the world with enough industrial power and resources to compete with the United States of America. This has already resulted in so-called economic wars between the two superstates. The economic competition also results in a technology and military technology race. And should a new World War be provoked by these particular issues, it will be most devastating for all humankind.

In the period preceding the invasion of February 2022, Chinese diplomats were very cautious when commenting on the situation. Nevertheless, it is evident that their sympathy is for Russia mainly and that Ukraine, as an ally of the Western world, is considered a potential minor threat at the regional level.

On the level of international relations, the Chinese influence comprised supporting Russia as a state and blocking further economic sanctions from European countries and the USA. In China's view, it was an episode of the opening stage of the political struggle with the West. This struggle also concerns the invention and adoption of new types of military equipment, including weapons of mass destruction.

The next point in Woodrow Wilson's program concerns the colonial claims of the opposing sides of the conflict and the right of self-determination for the colonized nations. This seems to be an archaic problem because there are no colonies in today's world and the problem mostly relates to the historical period of the First World War, but this is an extremely wrong impression.

First of all, there are postcolonial countries in the world today — countries that experience serious social and economic issues connected to the fact that they were previously colonized. This includes Asian countries and many contemporary states in Central Africa.

The separate discipline of humanities known as postcolonial studies emerged in the 20th century. It examines the different aspects of the problems that are experienced by the populations of the postcolonial countries. If not for the colonial politics of the European countries and the collision of their complex economic interests, the World War might never have happened.

It is not so clear, however, whether the colonies are completely a phenomenon of the past. Some researchers imply that the methods and rules of economic exploitation as well as political suppression and control changed drastically but still exist. Most of the postcolonial countries remain poor, underdeveloped, corrupt, and without any hope for bettering the situation in the near future.

It may seem that this is not only due to the deep impact of the historical events of colonization, but also due to continuing exploitation in the new globalized world. Colonialism evolved and changed its form — from direct military intervention to suppression — through the soft power of corporate culture, financial ties, and establishing the general culture of a region.

The topic of colonialism is also quite important for Ukraine. Researchers are quite cautious to call the sphere of interests of Soviet Russia a new colonialism usually, but it is evident that all the republics of the USSR were extensively exploited by the metropole. This has both economic and cultural consequences for contemporary Ukraine. In the UPR period, the same may be said about the Russian Empire and the territory of a future Ukrainian state.

The Ukrainian People's Republic's struggle with Soviet Russia may be presented as a national movement against the metropole, which was a widespread phenomenon for Europe in the 19th century and later, in the period preceding the First World War, in Africa and Asia. In one of the previous chapters, the ideological clash between Soviet ideology and Ukrainian nationalism was already discussed. Soviets saw themselves as freedom fighters and the UPR's nationalism as merely a capitalist "political technology" to hinder the world's Revolution.

It is, however, evident that Soviet Russia, especially in the later period, turned into an empire with all the consequences for the "colonies." It is again a dichotomy based on cultural differences, and, of course, there are no easy answers in such a debate. In the context of international relations, it is important to keep this dichotomy in mind because it is a defining detail for diplomacy.

In the contemporary period, Russia is still connected to neocolonial discourse. It can be seen in the cultural policy conducted on the annexed territories as well as the Donbass region. Ideological mythology, and especially the myth about the Second World War, is forcibly introduced into the cultural space and the education system of the regions. Sacred Ukrainian historical objects are destroyed, and the system of school education, especially history, is completely redesigned. That is a classical issue for colonial culture. It is not that different from the decommunization program of the Ukrainian government, but it seems that pro-Russian forces conduct their program on a bigger scale and more systematically. In this way, decolonization" is extremely important for both periods in view.

Unfortunately, Wilson's point about decolonization and the right of self-determination was never fully accomplished in real practice. African states and some parts of Asia are still experiencing internal conflicts and socioeconomical problems connected to their former colonial status. Russian and Soviet ideologists connect this to a sort of conspiracy theory by claiming that actual decolonization was just a political claim and that there were never plans to implement it for real. As for Ukraine, it experiences some of the problems deeply in the specific context of the post-Soviet territories.

Redrawing the borders and creating the League of Nations were mostly technical points of the program. The League of Nations, its failure, and consequent development of a new United Nations organization were already discussed. It is clear that with the development of humankind, the international relations will deepen and develop such that the emergence of such global organizations is unavoidable. It is social and political progress. Still, conflicts like the war in Ukraine and the ever-present fear of full-scale nuclear war raise questions about the effectiveness of such organizations.

Russia uses its influence in the international organizations to mitigate the consequences of aggressive actions. In the UPR period, the international community decided to support other political forces due to practical considerations of countering the Soviet Russia influence. That is a "diplomatic game" in a nutshell, and it is hard to see how to connect it to general morality. Humanism (and supporting the agenda of general human morality), however, is one of the core foundations of the United Nations (or, at least, it is so proclaimed). Otherwise, it would not be sociopolitical progress but extensive development of corporatism.

Preservation of territorial integrity is a very important political point, but it was violated numerous times both during the Second World War and in the contemporary world, including by the Russian invasion of Ukraine. It is evident that aggressive militarized societies that build their ideology on annexing territories and assimilating the population will always negate that principle no matter the economic and social consequences.

In the case of Hitler, most of the international community hoped to buy peace diplomatically. This was partially because of an appreciation of the devastation a new war would bring and partially because of the deep political influence of Nazi Germany throughout the world. The League of Nations did not really have a choice when most of the national states were neutral or supportive of Hitler's ambitions.

The United Nations was founded to avoid such conflicts in future. Nevertheless, there are still no realistic mechanisms to stop an aggressor like Vladimir Putin. Economic sanctions are not enough. Russian society is built differently than the democratic societies. Their values are not about economic prosperity. Due to extensive propaganda and mythologization of the war effort, the Russian population is ready for the militarized economy and great sacrifices on the frontline if this is the price to regain political influence. It is an imperialist ideology.

Analogies can be drawn with the early period of Soviet Russia. Industrialization that seemed to be another military campaign in the field of economics brought massive "casualties" — victims of overwork, social instability, and hunger (including the genocidal Holodomor in Ukraine). But it paid off in the sense that the political and military influence of the Soviet Union and the population supported such a course of actions.

During the beginning of the Cold War, the Soviet Union was the military super giant with the strongest army in Europe, but economically this country was very weak. It could not compete with the industrial power of the United States of America. Still, Stalin managed to mobilize the economy to create nuclear weapons and proved to be more than a worthy competitor in the Cold War. How can this be explained from a sociological point of view?

There is only one answer to this question. A totalitarian society is organized differently than a democracy on the deep sociopolitical level. It can afford to mobilize extreme amounts of resources and make enormous human sacrifices to achieve economic and political goals. This includes the situation when most of the citizens never even dream of prosperity and the elites are so completely closed that no social mobility is allowed.

The next point of Wilson's program concerns colonies again, and this problem was already discussed. Fair access to the raw materials is a little bit more interesting in the given context. Russia, due to its geographical position, has enormous natural resources, which it uses to achieve economic stability. Western analysts often warn about the danger of the Russian Federation using its resources to achieve political goals as well.

There were famous "gas trade wars" that influenced the politics of Ukraine in the 1990s and 2010s. In fact, this dependent economic status was a reason for many changes in the domestic policy of the Ukrainian state because the ability to make agreements with Russia about this problem was a very important factor. Russian authorities used it to manipulate regional politics.

And the economic ties of European infrastructure to Russia were one of the key points that influenced the decisions concerning the military support of Ukraine in the Donbass conflict. Putin implied he would cut the supply of energy resources to the European Union, which would bring a great crisis.

The last two points are extremely important as they relate to the core problems of international relations in the 20th century. Wilson recommends resolving all future conflicts with diplomacy, which is a humanist and progressive idea but utopian in nature, as was discussed before. But the last point develops this issue by proposing to introduce consequences for violation of the Fourteen Points.

This includes violations that start military conflicts. That would be a cornerstone concept for all the international organizations, including the contemporary United Nations. Although some of the mechanisms were invented, however, today's experience shows that they are not enough to control powerful players like Putin. The direct action of the international community, like during the Balkan Wars of the 1990s, also raises all sorts of ethical and political problems. The mechanisms of international control for aggressive authoritarian regimes remains the most important topic for future development.

It can be summed up that there are a lot of similar details in the diplomacy of contemporary Ukraine and the UPR. Both periods dealt with the reaction of the international community toward military aggression and the moral and political problems connected to it. Both conflicts prove that the international community is still underdeveloped, unfortunately, and cannot stop aggression from authoritarian leaders like Putin and Lenin. This fact emphasizes the important role of Ukraine for the region of Eastern Europe and peace initiatives on the global scale.

The extreme danger of a Third World War remains the most important global issue today. Studying the history of the previous context is useful for diplomatic efforts in the sphere of peacekeeping. Solving the "problem of conflict" is the highest goal for humankind.

7. Military Campaigns

There were a lot of military-related events and corresponding politics in both periods. The Ukrainian People's Republic made a diplomatic agreement with the Central Powers due to the objective military superiority of its neighbors and armed groups inside the country. The sad end of the UPR was also due to the military defeat. And none of the events of this period would have happened if not for the First World War.

ATO/JFO and the conflict with Russian-backed forces in general was one of the main topics in Ukrainian politics in the period of 2014–22. Only the COVID pandemic and the everlasting problem of corruption could compete with that on certain points. And after the invasion in February 2022, war and warfare are the main topic in Ukrainian media and public politics. This phenomenon has its roots in the history of the country.

It should also be mentioned that all the military campaigns and the politics of the next UPR period must be viewed in the general context of WWII. This great conflict was the trigger mechanism that started the Russian Revolution, the Bolsheviks rise to power, and the establishment of the Ukrainian People's Republic as well as the ensuing conflict between these new powers. Some of the previous chapters told the story of this context from the point of view of culture, but the military and political influence of the First World War was also enormous.

The First World War defined the geopolitics of the next period. It was the diplomatic relations that were established after this Great War that decided the fate of the Ukrainian People's Republic. The Western World decided to bet against the young republic. Poland and supporting its interests in the hopes of weakening the Bolsheviks seemed to be a more rational option at that time. Many details implied such a solution, including the organizational failures inside the UPR government. Some important factors were the objective circumstances of post-war Eastern Europe and even the world in general.

It is also quite hard to view the First World War without its implications for the start of the next great conflict—the Second World War. In a sense, these two conflicts are the cornerstones of the 20th century, and they define each other. In the previous chapters, the center of attention was the politics behind the conflict. In this chapter, it is possible to analyze the warfare of the First World War and its development in the Civil War in the former Russian Empire.

If the events of the Great War were defined by imperial ambitions, the Second World War saw the rise of totalitarian regimes that also had characteristics of the expanding empires but went far beyond. Historians often emphasize how irrational Hitler's plans of conquering the East were and how communist ideology played the same irrational role in Soviet society and Soviet military command during the war.

A lot was said about these new factors in the development of culture and society, and some more will be said in a chapter devoted to diplomacy and international relations. But all these factors also influenced how the army was organized, what ideology the simple soldiers had in their minds, and how the "society at war" concept worked in this period in general. The First World War was the event in the history of humanity that introduced the notion of the "total war" and weapons of mass destruction. These concepts would be developed in time and would define the Second World War and Cold War warfare.

There is a similar situation with the definition of the conflict by the context of the previous events in the period of 2014–22. Russian-backed armed terrorist groups started a revolt in the Donbass region. This military campaign was officially called ATO/JFO, but in the terms of troops and weapons used, it was one of the biggest armed conflicts in this region since the Balkan Wars of the 1990s. Ukrainian diplomacy in this period centered around the Donbass conflict and the annexation of Crimea, and all of these events were the consequences of the collapse of the Soviet Union and the ensuing internal conflicts in the emerging societies.

The tensions inside the Soviet Union themselves are mostly the legacy of the Civil War and the early years of the new Soviet state. It includes the nationalism of the occupied republics, including Ukraine. In the Soviet Union, this kind of ideology was suppressed and persecuted. In a period of "developed socialism," the topic of economics was added as well as the cultural differences between the modern society of consumption and socialist society, where the economic initiative and the according prosperity were impossible. These were all the pivotal ideological reasons for the subsequent start of war in Donbass.

In February 2022, everything changed drastically. The war in Ukraine after the beginning of the Russian invasion is the biggest conflict in Europe since the end of the Second World War. Only a few conflicts on the globe have involved more casualties and destruction than this war. It is not possible to assess it objectively, however, because the conflict is still ongoing. The only way to include analysis of these events here is to draw analogies to the ATO/JFO of the 2014–22 period and to study this conflict as the technological development of the previous one.

That approach aligns with the philosophy of history articulated by Wilhelm Dilthey. We take particular details and psychological characteristics of separate biographies to ascend to the general picture after the analysis. For example, we compare the Civil War in the Russian Empire and the First World War as well as the war between the Soviet Russia and Ukrainian People's Republic in terms of the technology of warfare used in the conflicts. There is trench warfare as opposed to mechanized warfare using quick maneuvers.

In a famous interview given to *The Economist*, Ukrainian Commanding General Zaluzhny, when commenting on the full-scale invasion after 2022, stated that, in the phase after the Ukrainian counteroffensive, the war entered the "trench warfare" period just like in the First World War. That is the material for the analogy with the particular situation in the period of the First World War and its connections to the other conflicts that happened in the UPR period.

The analysis is not simply comparing two events or two different processes. It is about establishing the complex connection between different systems where the analogy may be not that obvious. Precisely in this context, the psychologism in philosophy of history as well as the separate biographies of the key figures become important factors for the study.

In the previous chapters, different features of the Ukrainian state in both of the periods were compared—from society to diplomacy and international relations. Is it possible to compare the military histories of both periods? In the chapter devoted to analysis of the society, we doubted whether the technological difference is such a defining factor for sociopolitical change.

But what is evident is that military technology is a defining factor for warfare. It is very hard to compare the First World War and Second World War due to the difference in tanks, aircraft, and artillery. The war became more mechanized. Different tactics were used, and different strategies were used. Still, there are some periods in both conflicts that can be and are compared by military analysts.

People in the UPR era did not have the weapons we do nor the special equipment like drones and IT infrastructure. The speed of the campaign has changed as well as the tactics. Technology changes the way war is being fought as well as the impact on society. But the same was the case in the First and Second World War such that some analogies between local episodes and details can be made.

The First World War was the first conflict of such a scale on the planet. As its name implies, almost all the regions and countries of the planet were participating, and most did so directly. The reasons for the outbreak of the conflict were mentioned in the previous chapters—imperial ambitions of new global players, the rise of nationalism, and the big number of political and economic contradictions that were hard to resolve peacefully.

When we speak about the First World War, we usually mention trenches and warfare. For most of 1914–18, the war was waged by infantry hiding in those trenches. Big armies exchanged artillery barrages and direct infantry attacks to take and retake small pieces of the territory. Rapid advancement and the maneuvers of big armies in the classical sense occurred only in the first phase of the war. The same is true of both the Eastern and Western Front.

In this first phase of war, the Russian Empire had the initiative but eventually lost it due to internal social and economic tension. After first successes, Russian troops started to retreat deep into their own territory, which eventually influenced the proclamation of independence by the Ukrainian People's Republic and the Belorussian People's Republic. Previous chapters have already described the position of Russian historians that both these "political projects" were just new warfare tools used by Germans to distract Russian attention from the direct military action.

The advancement of military technologies influenced the picture of battle in this war deeply. It is the first conflict in the history of humankind that utilized artillery on such a monstrous scale. Machine guns had been invented in the previous century, but they also had a special new role in this war; they were decisive against direct infantry attack. And, of course, the invention of poisonous gas was a great shift not only in technology but also in the minds of people. It was the first weapon of mass destruction. The seeds of the Cold War and the constant fear of nuclear genocide were sown in the First World War.

The battles of the First World War were bloody on an unprecedented scale. Only the Second World War can compete with that. It was the first conflict ever to be called a total war. It was total mobilization of all the resources of the society, including human resources, total propaganda, and absolutely inhumane usage of those human resources. The new type of society, which can be called totalitarian, like the Soviet Union, Nazi Germany, and fascist Italy would have been completely impossible if not for the transformation of the world that took place in this period.

So, the conflict may be described as mostly "trench-related" warfare with major stalemates at the front line and awful casualties during direct infantry attacks and heavy usage of artillery. The Second World War still used horses and infantry, but the armies were much more mechanized, which allowed for quick maneuvers and tank *blitzkrieg* tactics. The first major successes of Nazi Germany on the Western Front were defined by the fact that the opposing side were preparing for the same type of conflict as the First World War. This proves that the First World War constituted a different warfare. Was the Civil War in the former Russian Empire the same as the First World War? The period between the World Wars was long, whereas the Civil War in Russia was almost the continuation of the First World War. Surprisingly, no.

First of all, the Civil War, despite involving all the nations of the former Empire, involved different numbers of soldiers as compared to the First World War. And it was not purely trench warfare anymore. In fact, both the White Movement and the Bolsheviks used maneuvers and quick relocation of the troops extensively. The railroad was used heavily, and the tactics were quite different from the First World War.

Another important difference is that the armies of both sides were organized on completely different principles. It is indeed true that many of the veterans of the First World War later joined the Bolsheviks, White Movement, or other factions, but their motivations as well as the strategy of their commanding officers were absolutely different. The Bolsheviks, for example, started their armed forces without officers using the system of the commissars and Party to control even the tactical decisions. This system proved to be ineffective, and the Bolsheviks later returned to the officer-based system. The institution of political commissars stayed relevant throughout the whole conflict, however.

The ideology of the armies fighting in the Civil War were also quite different from the preceding period. The society in general was tired of war and ineffective leadership. Bolsheviks used that feeling while proposing a new global alternative to the old way of life. That included the way the army was organized, as was mentioned before, and the new role of ideology in the life of the society.

The Red Army's purely military operations were accompanied by propaganda efforts and mass agitation. Talented orators and propagandists quickly rose in the ranks of the Communist Party. The Party, Cheka, and the Red Army were tightly connected, which is a very strange structure from the point of view of Western society. The soldiers were assured they were fighting something similar to a global Holy War and that they were morally superior to any enemy force. Sometimes propaganda failed, but there were often the cases when propaganda caused a wave of enthusiasm among the troops that allowed for serious military victories.

The White Movement also cannot be called the same structure as the tsar's army in the First World War. Most of the commanding officers understood that the old way of life was lost forever and that even if they succeeded in the re-installing the old tsarist regime, it would be a completely new story. There were also discussions about how the new society should be organized to avoid the repetition of the Revolution.

What can be said about the organization and the ideology of the armed forces of the Ukrainian People's Republic? It should be emphasized that organizing the army was extremely hard for the Republic's officials because most of the troops were tired from the First World War campaign. And as was already mentioned before, there was an intense competition between socialist and conservative ideologies. People were unwilling to join the UPR's movement as the national idea was underdeveloped in the society compared to other ideologies, including extremely popular Bolshevism. Still, there were soldiers who "voted" for the idea of the new independent republic.

There were also problems in the direct organizational efforts. Pro-Russian propaganda usually portrayed the army of the Ukrainian People's Republic as an unorganized gang that existed only due to German support and was quickly defeated in battle by the highly motivated and experienced Bolshevik forces. Even the successes of the Ukrainian armed forces are interpreted as episodic and mostly orchestrated by the third party. And, of course, such events as Bazar and the Battle of Kruty are completely desacralized.

Ukrainian historians draw a different picture with a place for honor and serious military operations as well as the talent and charisma of such UPR military leaders as Petliura and Skoropadsky. The important role of the Battle of Kruty for the national history of Ukraine was already emphasized. This difference in the depiction of these events and figures is a quite interesting case of the conflict of cultures. It has its purely cultural and ideological side, and, as this particular case implies, it has consequences even for warfare and armed forces. Cultural and ideological debates concerning this and other periods of the history of Ukraine continue nowadays and have great political significance in Ukrainian society.

Apart from the UPR, the Bolsheviks, and White Movement, other factions in the conflict also should be mentioned. Probably the most famous representative of the "third force" in this conflict was Nestor Makhno. He was an anarchist who framed his own military forces and in different periods was allied to different other players or fighting against them all.

At a certain point of time, he was an ally to the Red Army, and the Bolsheviks even considered him one of their commanding officers. But, in general, Makhno had his own political agenda. After his death as an emigrant, Nestor Makhno became sort of an icon for radical leftists and anarchists.

There were also numerous other factions that mostly had the structure and policy of criminal gangs. Those gangs were so powerful at a certain point of time that the UPR could not control the territories in which they were situated. There was a special term for this phenomenon—"atamanism." The independent leader of the armed group at that time was called an ataman, and the rise of those gangs to political influence got an according term.

Pro-Russian and pro-Soviet historians use that label to desacralize the Ukrainian People's Republic again. Their main idea is that the UPR government was never in true control of its territories except for the short period of German military support. Everything outside of Kyiv was actually under control of different atamans, and in fact, the UPR with its armed forces was nothing but another one of those gangs.

More to that, the phenomenon of atamanism also concerns discipline in the newly formed armed forces of the UPR. Pro-Russian criticism usually emphasizes that Ukrainian troops were unmotivated and that the different commanding officers were often independent leaders who had an agenda and interests of their own. That is a very serious kind of criticism implying the thoroughly ineffective organization of the Ukrainian People's Republic armed forces as well as the government in general.

That is very debatable, and this question is connected to propaganda's influence in historical science, which makes it even more complicated. Ukrainian historians have different opinions. There were indeed many organizational problems for the newly formed Ukrainian army, and atamanism was a major problem among them. Nevertheless, in general, there was an army of the Ukrainian People's Republic, and in most cases, it could support the order as well as conduct operations against foreign armed forces. The German support was valuable, but the fact is that the UPR could resist the pressure of multiple enemies many months after the Germans left.

The Russian historians' position here is extremely biased. Just as in the case of the Second World War, their criticism aims to attack the Ukrainian identity. If the Ukrainian People's Republic was a fake structure, then the ideology beneath it is fake as well. This has a strong application in contemporary politics as well. The attack on modern Ukraine and its national identity is the same, often using the same facts about the UPR era and other historical debates that were mentioned in the previous chapters.

Of course, that is not how professional historians work. They should be unbiased and politically neutral toward the events they research. Unfortunately, the current political situation implies that everything connected to the national identity bears with it a strong propagandist context. The continuing conflict makes history, as well as the humanities in general, a tool for propaganda.

And what about the conflict in Donbass in 2014–22? What was warfare like in that period? Some of the battles and key events of the campaign were already described in the chapter devoted to the political events of the two periods. Analogies between the Battle of Kruty and the Battle of Ilovaysk were drawn, but they mostly concerned the media side of the events. It is now time to analyze tactics and strategy.

First of all, the Donbass conflict in its active phase was far from the trench warfare of the First World War. Major battles of the ATO used a lot of armored vehicles and quick maneuvers as both sides were striving to encircle the forces of the opponent and cut off their supply lines. Artillery was actively used as well.

In the first days of war, the Ukrainian army actively used aviation to its advantage. The separatists did not have planes. Air strikes defined the initiative, but soon after, Russia supplied the separatists with powerful anti-air systems, and the advantage was lost.

During a period of relative peace with no major offensive operations being conducted, there was also a place for trench warfare. Just as in the First World War, there was a "trench against trench" situation. But there were no mass infantry attacks. Infantry groups usually performed storm operations on a limited tactical level and with the support of armored vehicles. There were also artillery duels.

In the last phase of the conflict, great importance was gained by a relatively new type of technical equipment—drones. Drones were used by technically advanced armies like the US forces in the Middle East many years before the Revolution of Dignity. Russian special forces also used them in Syria, but for the Ukrainian army in this particular region, it was a new technology. It changed the war drastically.

It is especially evident after the invasion of 2022 that mass usage of this technology changes the very rules of warfare. The invasion itself is not at the center of discussion, but it is useful to compare certain details of the warfare for the general picture.

In the last days of ATO/JFO, the technological initiative was with the Ukrainian side. It was the Ukrainian army that successfully used strike drones like Bayraktar on a tactical level. In the first phase of the full-scale invasion, Russian forces also started to use drones extensively. In later times, the initiative is with the invasion force for one simple reason—it can support far more powerful industrial production of the technical equipment.

Both sides blamed the other for human rights violations and jeopardizing the peace negotiations. Previous chapters mentioned the tragedy of flight MH17, the plane that was shot down by a missile while flying over the territory of the conflict. Separatists continue to blame Ukraine for specially devised provocations with civilian casualties, though the international court officially condemned separatists commanders for this act of terror.

During the Battle of Ilovaysk, there was another debatable moment. Ukrainian forces stated that Russian representatives agreed to allow the retreating forces safe passage, but they were massacred. This is another analogy with what happened near Bazar during the Winter Campaign in the period of the Ukrainian People's Republic. This makes this event another point in the political mythology of the period.

These ideological debates are very important because they constitute the informational and psychological conflict behind the purely military direct actions. The next generations will probably analyze these events just as we analyze the UPR period now. The war, no matter how bloody and dirty it is in reality, always constitutes the heroic epoch in the minds of the nation. Successes become legends, and the defeats create new martyrs. In this aspect, the Ukrainian People's Republic and the Donbass conflict are very similar.

What was the warfare associated with the period of 1917–22? As was mentioned before, it was different from the First World War, though certain technologies and tactics were still used. Railroads were used by all sides for quick maneuvers, and there were a lot of city battles in contrast with the trench war of WWI.

Another part of the analysis is media. Both conflicts have a serious significance for Ukrainian politics and political mythology. The Donbass conflict was at the center of attention of the Ukrainian media throughout the period of 2014–22. The Battle of Kruty and the Winter Raids were very important events for Ukrainian intellectuals in the period after the Ukrainian People's Republic. They are considered to bear a cultural legacy. This fact makes the media attention of both periods structurally similar.

The Battle at Donetsk Airport is similar to the Battle of Kruty in that both created an important cornerstone for the political mythology of Ukraine. The participants were heroized as symbols of the Ukrainian spirit. Both events also sparked heated debates among Russian and Ukrainian historians. The importance of these events for the ideology of Ukrainian nationalism was already emphasized in the previous chapters.

Nevertheless, media attention has influence on the war effort itself. In our contemporary world, media can define the impact of a military campaign on a society by mitigating the consequences, changing emphases, creating mythology, and actually changing the tactics and strategy.

It is easy to see how it happens in the more modern period of 2014–22. Classic propaganda is extremely important for the political side of the conflict. People are recruited for the direct actions through the spread of media narratives. Journalists' work is extremely important for the international context of the conflict. The media is also the main source of the informational and psychological war that are very important in the general picture of the hybrid war.

In 1991, French philosopher and sociologist Jean Baudrillard wrote his famous essay, "The Gulf War Did Not Take Place," in which he criticized the media depictions of the armed conflict in the contemporary epoch. According to him, the media changes the impact of military events on such a scale that we cannot consider contemporary warfare the same way people of other epochs did. The media defines the true political impact of each battle now. War is fought in what a French philosopher calls "a virtual reality," and supportive tools like media depictions take precedence over the tanks, bombs, and guns.

In many details, such a description of the Gulf War relates to the recent conflict in Donbass. The media also plays a pivotal role in this war. The Battle at Donetsk Airport can be a case study of how the media defines the impact and structure of an otherwise purely military event.

Does that mean that all that was said by Baudillard about the Gulf War also relates to the conflict of 2014–22? Partially it is so, but there are substantial differences. The Gulf War was fought by the United States of America, probably the strongest and technologically-best-equipped army in the world at that time. This had consequences for the media depiction of the campaign as the results of any military clash were predetermined.

The most attention was given to the political impact of each battle. Is the US army fighting for the right cause? Do the troops violate human rights in the region and to what extent? Is the war justified and are the aims of the campaign reached in the end of the conflict? Are the USA's adversaries legally and morally corrupt?

This is the phenomenon Baudillard was writing about in his essay. Ideological and informational questions about the war become more important than the war itself, and the face and impact of the conflict changes. It is still bloody and violent, but it bears completely different symbolic significance.

How is the situation with Ukraine and the Donbass war different? First of all, Ukraine is not the United States of America. We do not have those resources and that army, and, of course, each battle against the separatists backed up by Russia is not predetermined. The odds are not the same as in the Gulf War. Each side fights with all its resources and relies heavily on international support and diplomacy.

From the other point of view, it creates an interesting modification of Baudillard's theory. Media depiction becomes even more important. Each side of the conflict creates its own media campaign to aid direct military efforts. Ukraine presents its view with its associated concepts and political mythology, and separatists present a completely different picture. In fact, two different wars are fought, but they are media and PR wars while the direct military actions are more like a theater. It is just the source of the new content, while the main work is interpreting that content and continuing the discussion that is cultural at its core.

It is not easy to establish the same effects for the UPR period. Was it virtual, in a sense, too? The news about the events on the frontline were important, of course. But there were no social media where influencers could have an impact, and the speed of the spread of information was much slower. The media and propaganda still had their effect on the military, but it was a rather indirect effect.

One of those effects can be seen in the early historical episode of establishing a new government after the fall of the Russian Empire. It concerns the so-called Ukrainization campaign of the armed forces of the young republic. In the previous chapter, it was mentioned that the idea of Ukraine as a separate nation with its own identity was a relatively new idea spread mostly among the intellectual elite. The next stage required popularization of that idea together with political autonomy.

Most of the armed forces representatives were neutral in the best case toward the idea of Ukrainian nationalism. Many soldiers felt more connection to Russian language and Russian culture. The society was mostly disappointed in tsarism, but the sentiment for the metropole in the cultural sense was still an important factor. The mass of those who were still loyal to the "old Russia" joined the White Movement and became enemies of the Ukrainian Republic. Some of those "sympathizers," due to different reasons, stayed on the territory of Ukraine but were ready to "change flags" in time. Apart from that, Ukrainian nationalism had to compete with socialism and the newly spreading Bolshevism, which were popular ideas among the simple soldiers.

Many soldiers were agitated by the Red propaganda that was especially seductive to the ordinary citizens from rural areas. The Bolsheviks promised land ownership for simple peasants as well as social justice and a cease to social inequality. Soldiers were irritated by the fact that even during the biggest conflict in the history of humankind, where simple soldiers were dying and losing health, the elites of their countries were still living in wealth and prosperity. That was greatly emphasized by the Marxist ideology and propaganda that portrayed the First World War as a conflict caused by the bourgeois class and its imperial ambitions. In this picture, simple people were overwhelmingly deceived by the rich and powerful and losing their lives in a senseless slaughter, while the elite supported the status quo and its high status.

The leaders of the Ukrainian People's Republic, though autonomous from the remnants of the tsarist regime, were depicted as representatives of the same bourgeois class. That was an incredibly strong ideology and effective propaganda for the Bolsheviks. They created an absolutely alternative worldview and a complex system of political mythology, where the working class was surrounded by enemies and waging a sort of holy war for just order on the planet. This was empowered by the ineffective internal politics of the UPR, especially the mentioned politics concerning land ownership.

Some other soldiers joined other independent military factions on the territory of the Ukrainian People's Republic, like Nestor Makhno anarchists or simply armed criminal gangs with no political ideology. The criminal underground and its powerful influence became a very big problem in times of Civil War and after. It was a social issue for the newly established Soviet government for several years after the end of the military conflict.

Seeing those trends in the armed forces, Ukrainian officials decided to launch a mass campaign of "Ukrainization." The campaign involved a shift to the usage of the Ukrainian language and raising patriotic feelings as well as loyalty among the troops. It is a big question whether we can consider this campaign successful, but it brought major changes to the organization of the UPR armed forces and had a major impact on society.

This also proves that the army in the Ukrainian People's Republic was in a close interaction with the society and its trends, including cultural trends. "Ukrainization," no matter whether it was successful, would have been completely impossible if not for the preceding discussion of the national ideology among the intellectual elite. This also proves that the military sphere in the UPR had its informational and cultural side and can be viewed as being influenced by media and ideology like the Ukrainian army in the period of 2014–22.

So, there was a media side to the conflict of the 1917–22 period, and we also should take into consideration that the perception of those events itself is a very influential myth with political significance. In many respects, it is similar to the media aspect of the ATO/JFO. It is also important to remember that, with time, purely historical events become the material for the ideological debates that influence contemporary events.

The events before and during the First World War were partially described in previous chapters. The Russian Empire, despite its enormous resources, proved to be ineffective at waging military campaigns. Defeats at the frontline and the social pressure inside the country brought about the Russian Revolution. The Bolsheviks led a second revolt and started a profound reorganization of the whole of Russian society.

One of the main problems of the newly formed Soviet States was the former Russian colonies that proclaimed independence or strived for political autonomy. One of them was the Ukrainian People's Republic, but there were also problems in Georgia, Belarus, and the Middle Eastern regions of the Russian Empire as well as in Siberia that were mostly caused by the remnants of White Movement and local gang leaders who did not want to lose their newly gained power.

You can blame Bolsheviks for many things, but it is a clear fact that they were extremely effective at organizing a new social order and waging war, including the war against internal enemies. Cheka is often called the most effective oppressive political police organ in the history of humankind. The Bolsheviks managed to cope with most of the issues they faced in the early period of the Soviet state.

That was the end of the Ukrainian People's Republic, and the newly formed Ukrainian state emerged only in 1991. Decades later, Ukraine again faces extreme challenges concerning its security and even the existence of a Ukrainian national identity. This makes the period of the UPR great material for comparative study.

Different aspects of the warfare of the two periods were compared in in this chapter to the extent that the author's historical knowledge allows. Just as the psychologistic methodology in philosophy of history implies, it is very hard to consider the warfare of the periods in question as two big separate processes that should be analyzed like complex systems. Instead, there are similar details in different aspects and periods in both of the entities that make the analysis not only more complicated but also deeper and more interesting.

In general, the war between the Ukrainian People's Republic and Soviet Russia was quite different from the ATO/JFO, but there were strong similarities in political impact and media depiction of key battles that had their consequences for the political mythology. At certain points, the First World War was closer to the 2014–22 period, especially in terms of technology and tactics (trench warfare). And, of course, it is impossible to assess both periods without the preceding context.

In previous chapters, the preceding contexts mostly were connected to politics, but it seems that, in this particular case, the political context has its purely military subcontext. There would never have been the ATO/JFO if not for the Soviet Union's politics concerning the nationalism and national identity of its republics. The First World War defines all the next events up to 1939, when the Second World War started. This also includes military technology and tactics.

It can be summed up that this study shows the idea introduced by famous military theorist and strategist Karl Clausewitz: "warfare is just the continuation of politics using different methods." Politics defined and shaped the conflicts, while conflicts had their ensuing consequences for diplomacy and, again, regional policy. The ATO/JFO was followed by a full-scale invasion that was itself a product of the regional situation in Eastern Europe that was influenced by the Donbass conflict in particular.

The Ukrainian People's Republic and the events of the period between the World Wars was the historical context of the Cold War and the independence of Ukraine as the result of the Cold War. In this way, events and process in one particular country or region are connected on a global timeline and create global political history.

8. Ukrainian Society in 2014-22 and in 1917-22

It is evident that contemporary Ukrainian society is very different from its counterpart in the period of the Ukrainian People's Republic. There is a big set of reasons for that. Some of them, like the Soviet Union and its collapse as well as its continuing cultural influence, were already discussed. It is evident that the Russian Empire and the early stages of the Soviet state provided completely different contexts for the young Ukrainian state.

Some of these reasons lie on the surface, like the differences in technology, industrial production, historical and sociological context, and the situation in the international relations of the regions. Other are more subtle reasons connected to the cultural contexts and global politics that require a much deeper analysis of the situation. This particular chapter is devoted to these more subtle reasons and Ukrainian society in the period of independent Ukraine and the Ukrainian People's Republic in general.

Comparing the two periods is at the heart of the argument of this book. Different aspects of the sociopolitical life of Ukraine and Eastern Europe in general were analyzed to achieve this aim. Nevertheless, it is hard to compare just two periods chronologically as too many details are involved. There should be some guiding concepts. The society should be introduced both as a separate entity that requires specific methods and as a part of the political life of the region.

In this way, the society in general is at the center of attention in this particular chapter. It is also hard to define the required methodology because different schools in social philosophy and theoretical sociology view society from completely different points of view. The main detail here is how the general culture of two periods differ. The culture produces subtle sociological differences both through politics and ideological background.

The technological differences are the first point that stands out. Computers, communication technologies, the absolutely new role of mass media — these factors make our era very distant from the UPR period. They make both the sociology and the everyday life of citizens of Ukraine in two eras completely different. Or do they?

There were neither smartphones nor Internet in the Ukrainian People's Republic, but do the communication technologies define the differences between historical phenomena? There were other (more primitive) technologies, but the communication systems were already developed compared to the premodern eras. An analogy with classic sociology can be made here. Sociologists studied the classical historical periods to find the fundamental differences in how modern and ancient societies were organized. If we dwell in the history of the Middle Ages, then we will soon find out that there is a deep difference between that society and the modern one. It is explained by drastic changes in the economic and political system that changed the very nature of thinking in the next epoch.

Medieval people saw their role in society and nature differently. The class hierarchy in this society was profoundly different from the social hierarchy of modern society. People perceived religious faith and the very concept of the Divine absolutely differently. Some researchers claim that the very psychology of the person of this historical period was completely different from the psychology of a representative of the modern era. This also brings up the deep sociological difference between the societies of the two periods.

But is it the same with the more modern period of the UPR? Is it possible to say that such drastic changes occurred in the 20th century that a comparison of the two societies is very difficult or even impossible? It is not that the author denies the profound historical changes in this century, but the society after the First World War was in a dynamic state of continuing changes and thus much closer to the era of 2014–22. There is no great sociopsychological gap that draws a border between two eras.

The political system of this period resembles the contemporary situation. For example, there were newspapers and a lot of politics were public. There were democratic institutions and the corresponding democratic mechanisms. Modern technologies, of course, play a vital role in the speed of the changes. Information was spreading in the country much slower than today, but is this "speed of information" a decent criterion?

It might be said that the differences in the level of technological development concern not only the media and communications, but also production, the infrastructure, and the lifestyle. People use different products. People eat different foods and have different education systems. Due to historical reasons, however, these changes in Ukrainian society were not so fundamental.

The author does not strive to deny the role of modern technological infrastructure. Society indeed changed, but it is rather a gradual change than a completely new paradigm as with transition from the Middle Ages to the Renaissance. It is not the same as the described sociological research. Many social structures in Ukrainian society remain the same or very similar as they were during the UPR. The technology-based changes are more subtle than it seems at first glance, and what matters from the point of view of the methodology employed in this book are political and social relations. They influence society and not only pure technology.

The speed at which information spreads indeed means a lot for communication inside the state's society and the publicity of the politics and political actions. Only noble people engaged in politics in Antiquity and the Middle Ages not only because of the social and educational barriers but also because of the closed informational status of the world of the political elite. The social and legal systems also played their roles. It all changed only with the introduction of a new legal democratic system and the concept of public media. Of course, it was a vital part of the sociopsychological portrait of the era. People built their society differently because they thought and felt differently.

The first newspaper was a great invention and one of the first steps toward a democratic society. Nevertheless, as was already stated, there was some publicity surrounding the political world in the Ukrainian People's Republic and on an even bigger scale than in the tsarist Russian Empire. The Russian Empire was extremely rigid and aggressive toward democratic changes. In the end, this was one of the main reasons for its downfall. Russian society was not ready for the political changes. It fought any modernization until the emergence of the revolutionary situation.

Compare this to the period preceding 2014 in modern Ukraine. Yanukovich was the President, and the country was experiencing economic and political stagnation. Freedom of the press was rather more of an abstract concept than any real thing, and the situation in general was similar to the years preceding the UPR. It was the same revolutionary situation caused by ineffective policy. The Revolution of Dignity raised a lot of problems, but it also fostered great enthusiasm in the society throughout the country. The same was the case with enthusiasm in the early period of Soviet Russia and the rise of patriotism in the Ukrainian People's Republic.

There are, of course, not only similarities but also differences in the preceding contexts of these two Revolutions. Yanukovic was an ineffective authoritarian leader with a pro-Russian agenda, but he is hard to compare to the tsarist regime. And this is not only due to the historical differences, but also due to the deep structural factors that influenced the two contexts.

Yanukovich was dependent on Putin's Russia and his agenda was already mentioned, but in any case, Ukraine during his rule cannot be called an empire. There were no imperialistic general opinions in Ukrainian society, and the ultranationalist forces were in direct opposition to Yanukovich and his government. This fact defined the absolutely different approach in the domestic policy of the country.

The UPR period also had its subtleties. We compare the revolutionary events that preceded the emergence of the Ukrainian People's Republic with the Revolution of Dignity in Ukraine in 2013–14, but we also mention that there was another Revolution within the Russian Empire. The February Revolution and October Revolution that brought the Soviet regime into power had a major impact on Ukrainian society. The UPR would never have emerged if not for the downfall of the Russian Empire, but the political context of Soviet Russia and the new Ukrainian state were completely different, which eventually led to the military conflict.

And there were not just political and economic reasons for that conflict. The two societies—the new Russian-Soviet and the new Ukrainian—differed in the culture to such an extent that their unfolding conflict can be also called a cultural conflict. We have reviewed the influence of the socialist ideology in Ukrainian society as well as the changes that occurred in the perception of Marxism after the collapse of the Soviet Union. A major dichotomy was established between the Bolshevik ideology and the young nationalism of the Ukrainian People's Republic.

Ideologies constitute the political culture of the societies where they are established as dominant. This makes this topic central to understanding the societies of both periods. Socialism was a new, inspiring idea for the population of the former Russian Empire. This novelty played a vital role in establishing the Soviet regime in the country. In contemporary Ukraine, communism is usually associated with a very conservative worldview. Putin's Russia uses this conservative narrative, but it is fundamentally a different society than the Soviet Union.

The history of struggling ideologies and the new formats of this old struggle are very important for our understanding of the society of contemporary Ukraine. Nationalism is in conflict with both Russian nationalism and pro-Soviet conservatism. Culture, both national and Soviet, becomes an important part of politics and should be viewed in this context.

A critic might say that politics both on the global and local levels is not the only aspect of the life of the society that is influenced by the development of technologies. Smartphones really changed how people feel about themselves in their everyday life. Spheres that do not involve politics directly, like entertainment, are fully based on the technologies of the contemporary world.

Nevertheless, the scope of this book is devoted mostly to socially relevant details that mostly directly involve politics and sociology. It can be summed up that new technologies, including media, indeed greatly influenced our lives, but technology is not a defining factor for the political changes of the two periods in question. Meanwhile, politics and sociology are what matter for society in general.

Another reason for a different view on the factor of technology may be the economic situation in modern Ukraine. Unfortunately, the Ukrainian economy remains in the status of an economy of the developing, postcolonial world. There were both historical reasons for that, like the failing economic policy of the region during the Soviet Union era, and contemporary political reasons, like the corruption and ineffectiveness of the administrative efforts in the country after gaining independence.

These all were reasons that caused the situation of the infrastructure of Ukraine, as industrial production and business, to not really be in a state of postindustrial organization. In other words, the country, even in the period of 2014–22, was underdeveloped compared to Europe and thus closer to the technological and sociological situation of 1917–22.

During Soviet times, it was often speculated that drastic measures had to be taken to industrialize the territory of the country, especially the former territory of the Ukrainian People's Republic, which was mostly agrarian. These measures were indeed taken, which resulted in the series of catastrophic events that included the genocidal Holodomor. Though the economy of the former Russian Empire was severely modernized, and the Soviet Union was able to withstand the technological race with the West, this process was not as natural and gradual as it should have been.

It resulted in Ukraine never being fully modernized to the level of mass industrial production of the beginning of the 20th century. Many parts of the country remain agrarian, and without the obligatory period of industrial production, the country never made it to the postindustrial society of the 21st century. This has strong consequences for sociology.

Ukrainian society lives in the mix of the time periods. Kyiv's center is almost European, but most of the country is still in the 1980s Soviet Union era at best. Rural areas may, however, have even-less-modernized infrastructure. It can be said that those areas are stuck somewhere "near the Second World War."

These are reasons that concern technology and economics. The historical factors for the emergence of these differences mostly concern the period of the Soviet Union. The influence of the "red" culture in contemporary Ukraine is enormous, but it was already discussed in one of the previous chapters. It just needs to be repeated that this 70-year period polarized Ukrainian society, changed the attitude toward Marxist ideology, and introduced a lot of pro-Russian narratives into the culture of the country.

The Ukrainian People's Republic was also under the influence of the previous period of policymaking by the Russian Empire's administration. Though it is hard to compare the Russian Empire and the Soviet Union, they both were antidemocratic societies centering on traditional values and aggressive toward the national identity of the conquered nations, including Ukrainians. In a sense, the Russian Empire's policymaking brought about similar processes and problems for the UPR as contemporary Ukraine experienced in 2014–22. So, the preceding periods of the UPR, the Revolution of Dignity, and the revolutionary periods had strong similarities.

Maybe it is too brazen to say that history repeats in cycles. There are still deep differences between the UPR and the contemporary Ukrainian state. Nevertheless, the mentioned similarities imply that there is a lot to learn from the experience of the past for modern politicians and public figures. After all, the Ukrainian People's Republic eventually was defeated, and it is important not to repeat its leaders' mistakes.

Historians often emphasize the similarity of these two periods as it relates to the struggle for political and ideological independence. This context may be more subtle, but, in a sense, it defines the two periods more than just the difference in the levels of technology. Ukrainian society is influenced by the narratives of the constant struggle for independence and the preservation of the national identity. This can be seen in the mainstream media, political works, and cultural artifacts like literature and art.

The Revolution of Dignity and the subsequent events of annexation of Crimea and conflict in the Donbass region imply that the next period of the county's history will involve a lot of such struggle. Despite difficulties and obstacles, Ukraine mobilized the population and strengthened the national identity. In February 2022, these processes intensified. The war poses a question about whether a country will continue to exist or not. People with a patriotic agenda consider this struggle a central effort to preserving their identity and their way of life. Of course, it radicalizes society, which has both its pros and cons.

The concept of struggle was important for the Ukrainian People's Republic as well. In a sense, the Ukrainian identity was a completely new idea for most of the population, and it was modified and spread by a narrow elitist social group. This fact was also used by the Bolsheviks in their propaganda to emphasize that the vote for Ukraine was actually a vote for the society that encourages elitism and thus social inequality. Later, this political myth would transform into the myth about "fascist society."

Contemporary Russian propaganda also uses this "fascist" trope for the Ukrainian state. Now, it is harder to emphasize the inequality in Ukrainian society because the Russian Federation is actually built on even greater social inequality. The Russian elite are super rich. The population of Moscow and other central regions is relatively wealthy, whereas most of the country is extremely poor. This causes an interesting phenomenon, when propaganda starts to shift emphasis from the Bolshevik "equality and social justice issues" to a more cultural agenda, including the moral corruption of fascism, antisemitism, the mentioned conflict of the West, and the traditional values of the patriarchal society.

In some sense, it is a role reversal. During the events of 1917–22, the UPR built its ideology on national culture and protecting the identity and cultural heritage of the Ukrainians, whereas the Bolsheviks placed their bet on internationalism and socioeconomic issues. Due to a number of reasons, the Bolsheviks won that time, but this does not mean the internationalist idea is stronger or that Marxist ideology is more modern than a cultural agenda.

The Ukrainian People's Republic failed due to many reasons, including purely military and organizational issues. But an analogy drawn between a purely ideological "struggle" of these two factions is interesting. Does that mean that Putin's Russia is in a weaker position as compared to Lenin's Soviet Russia in his fight against Ukraine? The answer to that question may be incredibly complex and is connected more to the historical significance of Marxism and communism. For the purpose of this book, it is important to emphasize that contemporary Russia uses culture instead of international communist ideology. This makes the Donbass conflict a different type of war in the ideological sense.

Eventually, the UPR lost its struggle in the military and diplomatic sense because of the numerous reasons mentioned and discussed in the previous chapters, but it should be admitted that this period was extremely important and fruitful for the formation of the "Ukrainian idea." The language and culture actively developed, and the separate period of history that can be called completely national is an important determining factor. This can be seen from the fact that contemporary Ukrainian culture is a much more popular idea among the general population, and it has its political consequences.

In this way, the period of the Ukrainian People's Republic became one of the main myths for the Ukrainian nationalists throughout the 20th century, like the Heroic Era for later periods in ancient Greece. Several important processes for the formation of the political culture happened during this period of time. The Ukrainian language was the official language. Ukrainian culture was supported by the government and successfully developed and competed with other cultures. Separate national politics based on Ukrainian interests were conducted, including international politics and the creation of the Ukrainian armed forces. These all were factors that proved that Ukraine as a separate state and the embodiment of the Ukrainian idea can exist.

Prior to the UPR, there were only two sources for the justification of the Ukrainian identity and political idea: the era of the Cossacks and the cultural artifacts centering around the works of Taras Shevchenko. The Kievan Rus' period, as well as the Middle Ages in general, remain very debatable topics and targets for constant ideological attacks from Russian historians and propagandists.

Both aforementioned Ukrainian sources were connected more to culture and history than to practical politics. They were a foundation for Ukrainian national political theories in the 20th century. These sources remain extremely important for Ukrainian identity and politics nowadays as well.

The Cossacks and the era of political independence during the times of Bohdan Khmelnytsky are interesting from the historical point of view, but it is hard to consider them as the political model for the future idea of independent Ukraine. The political system of that time was archaic and non-democratic. This era constitutes the mythology about the warrior culture of the nation and is the source for epic stories about the past, which is an important factor for the development of the classic culture. For the same mentioned reasons, however, this period concerns culture more than politics.

The role of Ukrainian literature and poetry as well as the figure of Taras Shevchenko in particular was already mentioned in a previous chapter. His aesthetic ideas became a philosophical background for the kind of nationalism that seeks the roots of the state in folklore and simple people inhabiting the countryside. In some years, this ideology would evolve to the stage where Ukrainian intellectuals would form a concept for the political autonomy of the state. Through national identity, which is an important concept for Ukraine on a state level, Ukrainian culture defines the politics of the country in the 19th century. It is still an extremely important factor in contemporary politics as well.

The role of language questions in the political debates concerning Ukraine is enormous for today's society, and it would be a completely different issue were Ukrainian humanitarian culture underdeveloped. The development of poetry and literature caused the inception of the independent political opinion of the Ukrainians. Without the cultural artifacts of the 19th century, there would be no "political" Ukrainian nationalism.

The Russian imperial authorities saw that danger. This was why censorship of non-Russian-language works in the Empire was so strict. It also explains the oppression toward Ukrainian intellectuals and national culture in general. Sure, progressive ideas in a purely Russian context, including some advanced authors who wrote on political topics, were oppressed too, but there were no political barriers for politically neutral literature and poetry written in Russian. This fact was creating a great imbalance in the cultural situation in the regions of the country that had experienced negative consequences for the social development of local communities.

Soviet historians often cited the period of the Russian Empire as extremely oppressive toward socialism and ideas of social progress in particular, but their ideas bore great political significance and, after all, caused the downfall of the Empire. As for the censorship and the political persecutions of the intellectuals—they were even more fierce in the Soviet Union. Ukrainian national culture was proclaimed to be bourgeois and influenced by the West. Writers and poets were persecuted in the same way as foreign spies and saboteurs.

There was a brief period in the beginning of the Soviet era when development of the national culture was encouraged. In Ukraine, it got the name "Ukrainization." There were a lot of enthusiasts of this process even among the Ukrainian Soviet Party elite. After several years, however, the central organ of the Party in Moscow officially stopped this process and all the active enthusiasts and cultural public figures associated with Ukrainian language and identity were persecuted.

Why did this happen? Why did the official program of "Ukrainization" start and then end? Some historians claim that it is a feature of totalitarian regimes to start massive campaigns like this to find potential enemies. It may have also been the case that Soviet elites wanted to mitigate national opposition activity, but then the process became uncontrolled and frightening for the officials. In general, this incident is an indicator of how ineffective, irrational, and paranoid the Soviet political system was in general. A totalitarian regime's propaganda often provokes logical contradictions—the phenomenon that was described in George Orwell's famous novel. Citizens must learn to adapt and coexist with such contradictions in order to survive in this society. Of course, it has negative effects on mass psychology.

Both the Russian imperial officials and the Soviet Union officials claimed that the conflict of national cultures is a result of misunderstandings in regional politics and even "cultural sabotage." This claim is often backed up with the claims about the unity of Ukrainian and Russian people. In general, it is the same as the "Bismarck's Plan" political debate.

This and similar debates as well as the aforementioned "era of struggle" cause an interesting state for modern Ukrainian society. Culture and literature become the tool for politics, and national identity is both a moral and political choice, especially if you are young. Popularizing culture is an avenue for modern Ukrainian political activism, and in the period when ATO/JFO started, it became an even stronger trend.

Was it the same in the period of the Ukrainian People's Republic? Culture, and especially Ukrainian culture, was important in the UPR period as well, but the situation was a little bit different. Until the establishment of the Soviet state on the territory of Ukraine, the society was not as polarized as it is in modern Ukraine.

Ukrainian language and culture were even more rare in the beginning of the 20th century, especially in the big cities, and they were popularized mostly by a narrow group of intellectual elites. Of course, it had its imprint on the interpretation of the culture itself. Intellectuals of that period were searching for identity and political purpose among the national folklore and ancient history. Their view would differ from a simple worker, and this would have its implications for relations with the Bolshevik and Soviet culture in the future.

There were similar cultural endeavors among the Russian cultural elite and intellectuals earlier in the 19th century. "Simple folk people" or "narodniki," as they were called, explored the history of the country as well as the ethnographic material in much the same search for identity and political purpose. It had its contextual difference, though. Some of the participants of the movement claimed that their search was of a more spiritual kind that did not concern politics. But, in general, all these cultural endeavors were the early stages of a formation of a nationalistic ideology.

The interesting question here is why this process started in the Russian Empire so much earlier than on the territory of the future Ukrainian People's Republic. This chronological difference in the development of political ideologies in the two societies can also be seen in the case of socialism and other sociopolitical ideas. Ukrainian nationalists in the end of the 19th century were decades behind their Russian counterparts, who were in the "narodniki" stage in the 1850s and 1860s.

These purely sociological and cultural phenomena had their implications for the big politics, including the politics of the region. Would the history of the UPR be different had the nationalistic ideology been better developed in this particular region prior to the establishment of the Ukrainian People's Republic? Had the idea of political autonomy been stronger or maybe even the concept of complete political independence emerged earlier, the rules of the game would have changed drastically.

Despite cultural politics in modern Ukraine being far from the ideal, Ukrainian identity is a far stronger trend today than it was in the period of the Ukrainian People's Republic. Ukrainian literature and cultural products are far more popular among the general population today than 100 years ago. There is also a phenomenon absent in the Ukrainian past—the emergence of the Ukrainian segment of popular culture. Ukrainian discourse is now more than purely elitist or folklore related. It has its implications for the supporters of the Ukrainian national movement among younger people as well as modern national politics. And the Ukrainian national wing in politics is far more radicalized than even in the period preceding 2022.

Contemporary Ukrainian politics become more and more nationally oriented. They also concern the sociocultural policy in the state. The Ukrainian language is politically protected to a certain extent now. After the beginning of the invasion in February 2022, the situation changed even more. Russian cultural influence is considered now to bear political significance as well. Protecting the culture and heritage is closely connected to the proclaimed programs of decolonization and decommunization. The consequences of today's campaigns to rename the Soviet toponyms and isolate Soviet culture will be felt by new generations in the coming decades.

The UPR officials, in contrast, were really cautious about everything that concerned political independence and autonomy. Their ultimate goal was limited autonomy, which, of course, eventually would lead to complete assimilation by the Soviet government and society. It seems that this lack of ambition is in direct correlation with the level of the development of the culture.

The culture of the Ukrainian People's Republic was also heavily influenced by the culture of the Russian Empire. There were campaigns of cultural modernization in the country, like the "Ukrainization" of the army and usage of Ukrainian language in official documentation, but they never were on the level and scale of the contemporary decommunization and decolonization campaigns. More to that, Russian culture was never officially blamed for the Bolshevik military aggression, and many Ukrainian intellectuals with purely pro-Ukrainian political positions continued to develop ties with Russian culture and language.

This blaming, however, happened in the contemporary context. In February 2022, the question of the choice of language and culture became defined by politics. Still, there were some decolonization efforts in Ukrainian society in the preceding period as well. It is even more interesting to analyze the period of 2014–22 with regards to this aspect of social reality. The question of culture was still not polarized to that extent, and the hot debate in Ukrainian society about the possibility of staying culturally neutral was still ongoing.

In this period in particular, there were Ukrainians who considered their pro-Ukrainian position as not being in contradiction with the consumption of Russian language or Russian culture, whether it was popular singers or Russian classical literature. Today in Ukraine, the situation is much more polarized, and it is almost impossible to stay politically neutral in this context anymore.

It is an interesting fact that a very similar discussion was popular in Ukraine in the 19th century and for some part of the 20th century. The Ukrainian intellectual elites at that time tried to define what constituted the cultural features of the Ukrainian identity, and there were different opinions, including some that were quite radical.

A famous polemic public debate happened between the great Ukrainian writer Ivan Franko and his colleague, Lesya Ukrainka. The debate was about "radicalism" in Ukrainian nationalism as ideology. Ivan Franko considered himself and the Ukrainian intellectual elite from the Austro-Hungarian part of Ukraine radicals, and Lesya Ukrainka, who lived in the Russian part of Ukrainian lands, had different thoughts. At some point, the discussion defined "being radically Ukrainian" as the ideology of consuming and producing only Ukrainian content both in language and in spirit.

The discussion also mentioned that there are a lot of Ukrainians who know the language and take active part in developing the culture while also leaning toward Russian culture and especially progressive literature and philosophy. This is an interesting sociological and historical fact about the Ukrainian movement in the period prior to the emergence of the UPR. From one point of view, it may be the detail that implies that it is the same underdevelopment of the Ukrainian political ideology that caused some of the later problems with the political independence of the Ukrainian People's Republic. From the other viewpoint, it implies that the Ukrainian political and intellectual elite were quite tolerant and more consistent with Europe than the Russian radical nationalists.

There are also some practical consequences of these processes. Russian socialism and the Bolsheviks were formed in political debates and revolutionary activity throughout the second part of the 19th century. The ground was prepared for Soviet ideology and the new social order. The Ukrainian national idea and its supporting political movement were much younger. In the first stages of its development, it concerned literature and poetry more than politics or even any form of public activity. The UPR government was profoundly influenced by socialist ideology, which, because of the outlined reasons, was much more developed than the national ideology.

Contemporary Russian popular culture is older than Ukrainian popular culture as well. It seems that differences in national cultures cannot be assessed in the terms of "superiority" and "inferiority." Otherwise, it is fascism. Nevertheless, it is evident that the industry connected to the propagation of mass culture in the Russian Federation is much more powerful (in purely economic terms). And mass popular culture is extremely important for ideological struggles, especially when it concerns the younger generation.

Russian popular culture was dominant in Ukrainian society throughout the period of 1991–2014. Russian music was the most popular radio trend. Some Ukrainian bands were popular, but most of the young musicians kept in mind that the only possible success was connected to a relocation to Moscow. Russian literature, including intellectual literature, was prominent on the shelves of bookshops and public libraries. Ukrainian literature was considered to be a very special, narrow market, elitist in spirit but lacking in volume.

Ukrainian writers, especially those who wrote only in the Ukrainian language, were known and spread only among the enthusiasts of Ukrainian intellectual culture. This is an important fact because intellectual literature is one of the main indicators of the general status of the culture. People with the pro-Russian position often speculate that the influence of Russian classic literature is enormous in contemporary Eastern Europe and denying it would be a disaster for education in general.

That is a very debatable topic, and it is hard to say something rational here. Ukrainian enthusiasts usually claim that the popularity of Russian literature in Ukrainian society is artificial, caused by the continuous pro-Russian education programs of the Soviet Union and before that the Russian Empire. Pro-Russian debaters insist that it reflects an objective "market" situation as well as the general superiority of the "Russian discourse."

That sounds very radical and even fascist. As was mentioned before, culture cannot be assessed in terms of superiority or inferiority. Every culture is unique and precious. Russians condemn Ukrainians as dishonest and even nationalist oriented for introducing quotas and cultural heritage protection programs. Culture, however, is very important for the ideology, and in the contemporary situation, its role cannot be neglected anymore. The Russian position here is at least chauvinist.

Ukrainians also emphasize that consuming Russian-only content is an obstacle to deeper understanding of the Ukrainian intellectual discourse. There are extremely intellectual literature works in classic Ukrainian literature that are not exclusively related to folklore, but they are not that popular. Russian literature is a giant industry. Hundreds of the researchers are working on discovering and popularizing the Russian cultural heritage, whereas Ukraine lacks those resources. This also has an economic side to it — unpopular literature cannot be reprinted because there are not enough sale opportunities for it.

This situation is caused by several complex economic and political factors such that it is impossible to assess clearly as the phenomena that constitute the popularity of this or that discourse. In the beginning period of independence, little attention was given to the culture and ideology, which resulted in the mass expansion of the Russian and Soviet narratives into our public space. These were the main cultural reasons independent Ukraine faced the political problems and the new struggle for independence in 2013-14.

Did the situation change with the beginning of ATO/JFO? Some processes connected to the protection of the cultural sector started. Decommunization and decolonization were formed on the conceptual level, and the discussion about the role of the culture started in the public space of Ukrainian society. Nevertheless, as was mentioned before, there was a lot of reaction in Ukraine toward the new concept and the role of culture in the state.

Of course, in 2022, drastic changes in cultural policy started. The Russian discourse is blamed for the direct aggression, though there is always a way to deepen the culture-related program if it concerns decolonization. Changing toponyms provides an influence, but it does not address the deep influence of Soviet culture on the level of conceptual thinking. Those processes can only be influenced by a completely different level of decolonization program.

It can be summed up that the socioeconomic and cultural state of Ukrainian society are closely connected to politics and the military struggle. This fact makes the analysis of this sphere even more important than in a classical context.

Conclusion

As was stated in one of the introductory chapters, the period of the Ukrainian People's Republic and the period after the Revolution of Dignity and the start of ATO/JFO in Donbass have a lot of common features as well as a lot of dissimilarities. This makes the process of analysis and comparison of the periods in question not only much more complex but also much more interesting — and fruitful in new insights for the current political situation.

In some of the recent chapters, it was also stated that in the given circumstances, the analysis itself cannot be linear. This means that it cannot be a simple detail-after-detail comparison of the two periods. Different details in different subperiods should be considered separately and then incorporated into a more complex system, the general picture of the analysis. We did not take one period and compare it to the second step-by-step. Instead we tried to empathetically understand the period and its specific features and then compare these points to their counterparts in the second period. The counterparts can be mixed. They can differ, or they can bear a slightly different context. In this way, Wilhelm Dilthey's philosophy of history was the ideal option for this particular book.

Dilthey is a psychologist in his philosophy of history. He considers the biographical details and psychological characteristics of particular figures of vital importance for the historical events in which they take part. Apart from viewing personalities' biographies, it also implies that there is no need for linear-only viewing of the historical period. Particular details and influences may be considered important for the bigger picture without the fragmentation of the general view. Psychologism aligns with the non-linear view on the events, as the psychological characteristics of individuals are studied with this nonlinear methodology.

Wilhelm Dilthey was also interested in hermeneutics — a special philosophical discipline that deals with the analysis and interpretation of symbol-based cultural artifacts (mostly texts and documents). Hermeneutics can be also understood as a specific philosophical school that works with a special way of interpreting the culture of humanity. Empathetic understanding was part of Dilthey's method in his psychologistic approach to the philosophy of history. Empathetic understanding is irrational, based on intuition, and deeply concerned with the psychology of the individuals. And it is essentially non-linear just as was recently implied for the project of this book.

The book at its core also relates to hermeneutics. In this work, the author analyzes the periods in question and tries to understand the underlying mechanisms of the historical events as well as the "spirit of the time." The "spirit of the time" here is understood not only as a slight existential feeling of the particular time period, but also as an intrinsic intuitive feature of the era that allows for a unified approach to the analysis of the events and individuals of the period. Written documents are one of the main sources of material for such a research study, so it is the same as historical science but with a special place given to the psychological intuition of the researcher. With a hermeneutical method, we try to find the true nature of the phenomena through empathetic understanding of their key aspects.

Hermeneutics is all about understanding and interpretation. As a philosophical discipline, it started in the second part of the 19th century. The need to understand the documents and events of the past, however, appeared in human culture much earlier. The first attempts to do hermeneutical research concern the text of the Bible. Purely philological hermeneutics appeared much after the application in theology.

That is a very interesting detail that also has its roots in the history of the society of that period. For medieval society, the need for the right interpretation of the sacred text was enormous because the Church defined the life of the society. That was a period of dominance of one global text. The role of the Bible was enormous for political and social history.

In contemporary times, the situation is quite different. Religious rituals and sacred texts are still an important part of culture and everyday life, but they are not as definitive as in the Middle Ages. The modern global world is multicultural, and different religions compete with each other in the public space, which was impossible to imagine in the previous epochs. Modern society is also, at least in some places, secular, allowing for atheism and independence from religious organization in public policy and administration.

In a sense, we live in an epoch when reality is defined by the multitude of different texts—from religious to fictitious and journalistic—but none is the main text. What does this mean for the culture? The reality got much more complicated. For the medieval human, the questions about the purpose of life and similar topics were all defined and interpreted by the priest, who used the Bible as the source for his interpretations. Philosophy and logical speculations were only for the extremely privileged educated minority—certain monks and nobility.

The Middle Ages are also famous for their different understanding of the individual and their general place in society. Historians often emphasize this fact in its particular relation to the texts. All the texts that did not relate to theology were considered technical, and theology was only the support for the aforementioned main text of the Bible. This also raises the problem of authorship.

Many medieval texts are anonymous because there was no contemporary concept of the author. Authorship was not viewed as something advantageous, and more to that, mentioning the name of the author of the document might have seemed to be the sin of vanity. This caused the situation that most of the texts of that period are anonymous compilations.

Today, you can still go to the priest for answers, but he and his interpretations do not play the same role as they played in earlier times. You have to think for yourself and make your own choices, including the moral and existential. Texts may help you, but most of them contradict each other. There is no dominant codex anymore. These facts make contemporary reality much more complicated for the individual. This also relates to history in general and the purpose of this book.

Historical research is one of those "competing texts," so the described humanitarian context is also the context for this particular book. The work deals with the interpretations of the symbols and events of the past, which is a vital part of understanding the reality. This is a strong connection to hermeneutics as a discipline.

In one of the introductory chapters of the book, the problem of the aforementioned "spirit of the time" was viewed. It was claimed that there is an intuitive atmosphere of each time period that can be perceived only through empathy. Meanwhile, this "spirit of the time" is extremely important for a true understanding of the historical period and the events that occurred. The methodology of empathetic understanding was used many times throughout the text of this book.

The "spirit of the time" concept and hermeneutics are important methodological concepts for study of the classic historical periods, like the Ukrainian People's Republic (1917–21), but the second period in view is the recent past—the period of ATO/JFO (2014–22). Is it possible to claim that there is also a "spirit of the time" for that period? The fact is that most of us lived through this period and do not have the "historical distance" to judge about events and processes as historians, without emotions and moral evaluations.

It is also a question whether, in light of this fact, we can assess the events of ATO/JFO using the same methodology as the UPR period. There is definitely a "spirit of the time" for the period of 2014–22, but the real problem is how to assess it. If we are participants in those events, then is empathy even rational?

The absence of the "historical distance" and the "spirit of the time" are two different problems. "Historical distance" relates to the old problem in historical science, the professional ethics of an historian. A historian cannot be affiliated with any political faction that was active during the period they research. That is an obvious rule, though it is quite hard to follow, especially when it concerns the national history in circumstances similar to those in contemporary Ukraine.

Throughout the book, weighty debates between pro-Russian (pro-Soviet) and Ukrainian historians were mentioned several times. These debates bear a strong political significance because different periods and facts in Ukrainian history can be interpreted either as justification of the Ukrainian national identity or as justification of Russian claims about the dependence of Ukraine on their culture. This makes these debates very ideological and even political, which accordingly makes the work of the Ukrainian historian much harder because they need to avoid the politics and concentrate on the science.

An additional context that influenced these processes is the recent invasion by Russia in Ukraine, the start of a full-scale military aggression, and the political decisions made concerning cultural policy and historical science in particular. This context is connected to the program of decommunization and decolonization that was already begun in the Ukrainian state after 2014 but became much more active after February 2022. The program is about getting rid of the Soviet and Russian legacy in the public cultural space of Ukraine and reclaiming the authentic national cultural heritage instead. Culture becomes an important part of political and military struggle.

This program was commented upon in one of the chapters of the book and even compared to similar processes in the Ukrainian People's Republic. The UPR had a similar campaign of Ukrainization in the armed forces of the state and the public cultural space as well. It was emphasized that, in the time of the Ukrainian People's Republic, the ideas of a separate Ukrainian national identity and even political autonomy were not that popular among the population, which, of course, had its political consequences, including the negative circumstances for the existence of a young republic.

Maybe if the UPR had more time and a little bit different (more effective) cultural politics, then the events would have turned out differently. Culture is a background for the political consensus in the society. Unfortunately, the practical consensus in the society of the Ukrainian People's Republic was not in favor of independence.

The consensus had its implications for economics, public politics, and the armed forces. Ukrainian society was disorganized, fractured, and under the heavy influence of the anti-national political narratives. And all these issues relate to culture and cultural policy, so it is the same issue for both periods of Ukrainian history in question.

In general, it should be noted that the work of a Ukrainian historian in the contemporary context becomes much more subtle and complex. They should take into consideration their own prejudices as well as the political context and professional ethical standards. That seems to be true of any historian who works with the period after the First World War, but in the Ukrainian context it is even more important and pressing because even the medieval period of Ukrainian history is material for the aforementioned ideological debates.

As for the "spirit of the time" problem, we have established that there is an intuitive side to the most recent time periods, but we cannot decide if we have the right to assess them as we do the distant past and if we can use the same methodology for this purpose. To answer these problems, we should emphasize that this book is not only an historical work, but also a work of political philosophy wherein historical periods are compared to reach new insights concerning politics and policy, including contemporary politics and policy. That is why the analysis pays attention to the separate details and subprocesses in a manner outlined just as was stated before.

In this sense, the work is opposed to the classical philosophy of history that is represented mostly by Hegel and his conception of the Absolute Idea. This conception proclaims that all the history of the world is a development of this Idea, and the highly organized society is the highest form of historical development. Hegel's idea of such an organized society is a state with strong authoritarian rule and strict laws, what we would call a "police state" today.

Do we avoid Hegel's theory only due to the proclaimed usage of the irrational methodology of the psychologist Dilthey? Not entirely. Dilthey's empathetic understanding aligns with the idea of this book due to the methodology employed—the non-linear analysis of different details of the two periods. There is no direct criticism of Hegel and his ideas in this work, but the very idea of the book is opposed to his philosophical system.

That does not mean, however, that the author considers Hegel's system of the philosophy of history false. It was made clear that Dilthey's ideas are more suitable for this particular research, but Dilthey himself, though developing in a different direction, did not completely deny Hegel's ideas. After all, he wrote one of his psychological historical research works about this great, idealistic, German philosopher. Neither was Dilthey's work a direct criticism of Hegel's concept of the philosophy of history.

In the beginning of the book, it was also claimed that Hegel's philosophy of history was a source for the school of philosophy of law that puts the state governmental system at the center of human existence and is later associated with big, bureaucracy-influenced states like empires or even the totalitarian regimes of the 20th century. After all, it was Hegel's philosophy of law that was one of the main cornerstones for the later philosophy of Karl Marx.

But this does not make this philosophy automatically bad or false. It just emphasizes that Dilthey's approach may be more suitable for the phenomena at the center of attention in this book. After all, Hegel is quite an important philosopher on the scale of the world's history of philosophy and culture. More to that, his philosophy may be a suitable tool for better understandings of the societies that relate to this kind of philosophy of law, like Soviet Russia and contemporary Russia.

Ukraine is not an empire and, though it has many problems in domestic policy and economics, is a more democratic state than contemporary Russia or the Russian Empire. In this way, there is another reason to use Dilthey's methodology in this particular work. It is more suitable to the subject of the research.

There is a separate chapter in the book devoted to the comparative analysis of the societies of contemporary Russia and the Soviet Union in its earliest period of political history. It is important to understand this neighbor of the Ukrainian state because, both in the period of Ukrainian People's Republic and in the period of the ATO/JFO, this state was the main aggressor and the main factor of destabilization inside Ukrainian society.

The mentioned chapter provides the regional context both for contemporary Ukraine and the Ukrainian People's Republic. The history of ATO/JFO is mostly the history of international, diplomatic struggle against the Russian Federation with a background of direct military action against its proxy powers. All these processes are connected to regional security in Eastern Europe in general. The UPR case also involves the consequences of the Civil War in the former Russian Empire as well as the young, radical communist ideology. Both these issues were addressed in the text of the chapter.

Of course, there were more factors influencing the end of the Ukrainian People's Republic than just Soviet Russia or the Bolshevik political program and propaganda, but these later factors were decisive for the whole situation. That is why such great attention is given to these particular issues in the text. There is also a strong connection to the contemporary period, which makes this chapter even more important.

As for the general project of the book, the macrohistorical, big picture, political, and geopolitical context of both periods was given, and then the particular points of politics and society were analyzed and compared. Among those points were the biographical facts about key figures of the two periods as well as the description of their involvement in bigger historical events. From the particular local stories, we move to the global story just as the methodology we employ recommends.

The second chapter of the book, entitled "The political events in the Ukrainian People's Republic and contemporary Ukraine," is devoted to the analysis of the main events of the two periods and the bigger picture, whereas all the next chapters delve into the particular details of these periods. It is the longest chapter of the book, and while most of the material from the other chapters concentrates on the society and the general context of the epoch, the main attention of the second chapter is on the political events that constituted the periods in question.

Why is that so? Why is politics at the core of the book? This question is also addressed throughout the text of the work. Politics and domestic policy encompass the essence of the historical events and thus constitute the development of society. For a reader of this book, it may be obvious that the main emphasis is given to the issue of social development rather than military history. There is, however, still a chapter on the military history of the periods in question.

The battles and other military-related events are viewed thoroughly in the book. The most attention is given to the Battle of Kruty, the Battle of Ilovaysk, and the Battle at Debaltseve. Though lacking military education and experience, the author analyzes the battles from the point of view of cultural and social impact. The concentration is on the media's impact and the political mythology that these events constitute.

Jean Baudrillard and his philosophical concepts are mentioned several times in the text. Baudrillard studied contemporary society and the role of media in the formation of social reality. He gave special attention to contemporary military conflicts, including the Gulf War. His idea is that in the given circumstances, the media campaign is so important that it not only modifies the direct military actions, but also changes them drastically. In fact, the media becomes more important than the warfare itself as it constitutes the mission of direct action, its social impact, and political consequences.

That is especially important for the modern type of war but also has its roots in the period of the Ukrainian People's Republic, as is shown in the corresponding chapter. People supported this or that political faction based on their ideology and public image. Culture was incorporated into that ideology, especially in the case of the Ukrainian national idea. The ideological debates and the national identity were an important background for the direct military action already taking place in that period, and the connection of these two spheres only strengthened in the contemporary world.

A separate problem is the historical and ideological perceptions of the events of the UPR period in later chronological periods, including contemporary Ukraine. As was said before, the period of the Ukrainian People's Republic is extremely important for the historical science of the independent Ukrainian state as well as the national identity. This makes many topics connected to this period very debatable, especially when it concerns politics. So it is evident that the UPR is part of Ukrainian political mythology.

Pro-Russian historians use the exact opposite description for that period in Ukrainian history. Public figures that are depicted by Ukrainian historians as heroes, as well as the Ukrainian government of that period in general, are vilified by their opponents. The Ukrainian People's Republic is introduced as ineffective, corrupt both morally and politically, bourgeois, utterly artificial, and created as a separate national entity only as a tool of European influence in the region.

Russian propaganda here has two main aims. The first is to attack the very idea of Ukraine as a country that possesses a separate national identity. The second is to justify the actions of the Bolsheviks and the common future of Ukrainians and Russians in the Soviet Union. There are sometimes peculiarities in the ideology of the Russian propaganda concerning the communist ideology and the relation to it. Contemporary Russia really appreciates the Soviet imperial legacy but not the system itself. Nevertheless, these are all peculiarities, and in most cases, pro-Russian propaganda is well-coordinated.

Much attention in the different chapters of the book was given to this exact topic—the ideological controversy between nationalist-oriented humanitarians and pro-Russian (pro-Soviet) humanitarians as it constitutes the ideology of the conflict and defines its practical aspects. The conflict, at its core, is culturally defined. That is an evident fact. Another interesting question is whether the UPR's wars with the Bolsheviks and the war in Donbass are the same conflict or different ones.

This question concerns one of the main aims of the book—a comparison of the two periods. Can we call the contemporary pro-Russian forces the exact legacy of pro-Soviet forces and Bolshevik political ideas? This question is addressed in the chapter devoted to comparing contemporary Russian society and the society of the early Soviet period. This chapter ends with a statement that Putin's Russia indeed relates to the communist imperial past and ideology as it is "politically profitable" but is not sociologically close to the society built by Vladimir Lenin.

It is doubtful that those two conflicts are the same. This may seem like negative evidence for the purpose of the book at first glance. If they are not connected in that manner, then why compare them? It was concluded, however, that they have a deep intrinsic relation and many common details and features that make the purpose of comparing them even more important.

ATO/JFO and the Revolution of Dignity are also very important for the Ukrainian national identity. It is also a time of great heroes and sacrifices, but it is perceived as the contemporary time, without the "historical distance" that was already mentioned earlier in the text. This makes it hard to assess these events scientifically, but the key figures are still considered important. It is evident it will become a vital part of Ukrainian political mythology with time.

The Revolution of Dignity is already a very important part of the national idea. It is usually associated with the pro-European vector of development of Ukrainian politics, culture, and society. Europe is itself associated with freedom and prosperity and a different "civilization choice" than Russia.

President Yanukovich's actions of canceling the previously agreed course of integration into the European Union is considered an act of treachery. Euromaidan with all its struggle and numerous sacrifices of human lives is considered a heroic and sacred act. The subsequent events of the annexation of Crimea and the start of ATO/JFO are usually viewed as the logical continuation of the Revolution of Dignity.

Some attention is given to the more global issue that encompasses the previously mentioned concepts as its parts. This is the global coexistence of the civilization of the West and the civilization of the East. Russia and Europe are opposite possible choices for Ukraine that mark a more global choice between these two parts of the world. That is a very complicated issue that relates not only to the politics—regional politics and even geopolitics—but also to the philosophy of history as well.

Russia is not a global East but rather a representative of it just as Europe is the representative of Western culture. Russia and the Soviet Union are associated with eastern views on the role of individuals in society, eastern methods of administration in politics and business, and, of course, eastern values. The East is a great culture (just as the West is), but it brings its drawbacks like despotism and disregard for human life and human rights.

These values represent a more patriarchal and traditional conservative view on how society should be organized. Russia actively uses this conservative approach in its propaganda and strategic communications. The Western world is claimed to be morally corrupt and not only corrupt in a political sense. In particular, this can be seen from how the two sides interpret the problem of the LGBTQ communities and social mechanisms connected to the traditional family. Eastern civilization is for the patriarchal model of the family and the corresponding understanding of sexual minorities. The West, for its part, represents respect for different minorities and their protection through the mechanisms of democracy.

This has its consequence for the status of human rights in the politics of different countries. The eastern understanding of the role of the individual and personality in the general political order is incompatible with the very notion of human rights. Authorities are expected to continue their activity no matter the consequences for the simple citizens. The purpose of the state and society in general is what matters more. In extreme cases, it brings the aforementioned disregard for the greatest Western value—human life.

Russia presents itself as the protector of the traditional conservative values and classical social institutions. There are a lot of people in Ukraine who support this "conservative vector." This is due to historical reasons—the territory of Ukraine was long under the influence of empires that employed a thoroughly traditional approach to interpretation of this sphere. It makes Russian propaganda extremely effective in this particular case, which has its political consequences.

The process of integration of Ukraine into Western society was made harder by many active supporters of the pro-Eastern vector in the society of our country. That is a sociological phenomenon typical for societies where different systems of values collide. Similar processes happened in Afghanistan during the Soviet occupation—the traditional religious part of the society opposed the atheistic communist agenda. Just like most of the conflicts on the globe throughout history, the war in Ukraine in both periods concerns cultural collision.

This, however, makes the conflicts even more complicated for a diplomatic resolution. When war starts on the globe, the international community tends to try to establish its legal (in the system of international law and relations) and moral status. It is evident that, in a war like the Second World War, there is a particular aggressor (Nazi Germany and its allies), and particular decisions of the international court condemn the crimes against humanity and the violations of rules of war.

In fact, the Nuremberg trials not only established the local and international legal systems, but also were a great influence on the morality and moral codes of humankind. Previous chapters mentioned that the first half of the century gave rise to totalitarian political regimes that interpreted the value of human life and its purpose in a new, instrumental way. That was an enormous influence on how we understand the world and the place of the individual. This influence, however, cannot be called positive.

The Nuremberg trials can be called a late reaction of human society to the changes and processes connected to the horrors of totalitarianism and the World Wars. Despite the great losses of the previous conflict and many compromises, these trials officially established that there is still a morality in the world, that there are still powers of order that struggle with the chaos and injustice. That was also sort of the founding event for our contemporary political and legal reality.

The Soviet Union did not collapse right after the Second World War, and the tensions in the world order were followed by the Cold War and numerous regional proxy conflicts. This situation established not only the new political situation on the globe, but also a new framework for understanding the reality, the contemporary situation of the individual in the world. All of the conflicts in a new globalized world were viewed as part of the unified general story of the struggle in the bipolar world.

Many people claimed that the victory of the Second World War over Nazism was not complete because the Soviet Union, which also committed crimes against humanity, was still extant and using all sorts of political persecutions against its citizens. This problem is extremely complex because it involves both complicated moral problems and international relations and politics.

The consequences of this situation are seen from the contemporary Ukrainian context. Pro-Russian and pro-Soviet debaters use the myth about the Second World War as a special, sacralized, moral-defining event as one of their main propaganda tools. Ukrainians are depicted as traitors who sided with absolute evil during the active phase of the struggle. That is very effective because it automatically makes the opposing side morally flawed.

The myth about the struggle against Nazism and the role of the Soviet people in this struggle was such an important concept in Soviet ideology that, at a certain point, it overshadowed the October Revolution and Lenin's socialist project. This concept became so ideologized it can be called the element of morality on the territory of post-Soviet countries. It goes deeper than political ideology, and that is why any attempts to reason about this myth are mostly futile; they are met with aggression.

After the collapse of the Soviet Union, the situation changed drastically, and the world's security remained stable for some time. Nevertheless, in recent years, it seems evident that the danger of a new World War with mass usage of nuclear weapons is again an actual issue. Today, the most attention is given to China and its geopolitical ambitions, but Russia and Putin are still important factors. Some of the previous chapters of the book cite the collapse of the Soviet Union as a defining event for the ATO/JFO period in the history of independent Ukraine.

Most of the social and even military conflicts on the territory of the post-Soviet country were caused by issues that existed and were cultivated in Soviet society. In the case of independent

Ukraine, these issues are the question of the language and the struggle of the cultures. That is a typical situation for societies that were under the influence or were colonies of the empires. Similar issues were faced by the population of Central Africa, which led to a devastating war.

The conflict in Donbass became inevitable as soon as Putin proclaimed his neo-imperial political program. In this way, regional politics had cultural differences and the clash of cultures as its vital background. If there are problems in the cultural landscape of the region, then conflict, including overt military action, will inevitably follow. Still, it makes the project of the cultural and historical analysis of these issues even more important.

This brings us back to the period of the Ukrainian People's Republic and the importance it bears for the contemporary political situation. The UPR existed long before the Second World War and the establishment of the according myth. In our previous analysis, we also came to the conclusion that we cannot state that the conflict of 1917–22 is the very same conflict as in 2014–22. There is, however, a strong similarity and influence of this previous period on the next events.

The Russian Empire in the period preceding the inception of the Ukrainian People's Republic was a more traditional society, where it would be impossible to imagine the same problems concerning the family as an institution. Was the Russian Empire the same representative of Eastern culture as the Soviet Union and contemporary Russian Federation? Most probably, yes.

The opposition of East and West is present in the culture of that period, including Ukrainian literature. Maybe it is not as persistent as it is now, after the Cold War, but European culture and society are compared to the society and culture of the Russian Empire many times. The Russian Empire had many features of a state heavily influenced by Eastern values and Eastern systems of social institutions.

Russian aristocracy only had their serfdom canceled in 1861, long after the similar processes in Europe. Peasants, however, were still in great economic dependency on the aristocrats, which created a serious internal social pressure. Eventually, this social pressure was one of the main reasons for the October Revolution.

This serfdom social issue is usually described as part of Eastern political influence. The strict position toward the citizens and political elitism and the disregard for those with no influence in the society is typical for an Eastern society. Ukrainian historians often claim that the despotic type of political administration used in the Russian Empire is influenced by Moscow having been part of the Golden Horde.

This point about the influence of Eastern civilization on the Russian Empire is often used by pro-Ukrainian historians in the debates concerning political questions surrounding the problem of relations between Russia and Ukraine. This point became especially important after the Revolution of Dignity as the European and Western values in general were proclaimed to bear importance for the future of the Ukrainian state.

In this way, we can see that the history of Ukraine in general, as well as such important periods as the UPR, is part of contemporary politics, ideology, and propagandistic messages. And there is definitely an intrinsic connection between what was happening during the Ukrainian People's Republic and what is happening in contemporary Ukraine, including the events that unfolded after the Revolution of Dignity.

After the beginning of the full-scale invasion of Russia in February 2022, the narratives in the ideology of Ukraine also shifted. Now, the main idea is about the heroic struggle with statehood and the national identity at stake. Still, the Revolution of Dignity and the period of ATO/JFO are very important supportive concepts. Should Ukrainian identity survive the war, there will be another shift and the events from 2014 on will be considered as a unified series of episodes of the political struggle for independence.

Previous texts retell the facts that are analyzed in different chapters of the book as they concern the purpose of the work in general. Some of the core concepts of the book were highlighted in the unified system. It is time to describe the general structure of the book and conclude.

The first chapter, called "The idea of analysis," introduces such core concepts of the following text as empathetic understanding and the psychologism of Wilhelm Dilthey; "spirit of the time;" and the comparison of two periods both as history and as political philosophy.

The chapters "The political events in the Ukrainian People's Republic and contemporary Ukraine" and "Bolshevik Soviet Russia and Putin's Russia" were described in detail in the previous text. The chapter "Contemporary ideological debates" is devoted to one of the key concepts of the book—how history and ideology influence contemporary politics through active discussion.

There is no question that historical discussions are important for politics, but Ukraine is probably the country where this importance is highest due to sociopolitical reasons. The "Major shifts in power" chapter studies some of these reasons and the consequences that the February Revolution and Revolution of Dignity had for their time periods. The "Ukrainian society in 2014–22 and in 1917–22" chapter is also devoted to these many factors but with more attention to the aspect of social factors.

The "Diplomacy and international relations" chapter focuses on the international status of Ukraine in the two periods because diplomacy was a defining factor for the Ukrainian People's Republic as well as quite an important factor for Ukraine in the period of the ATO/JFO. Much of the chapter about the military events was also revisited in the above text.

I would like to conclude by stating a hope that my book will be of interest to historians and people interested in Ukrainian politics. As was claimed in the introduction, it is not only pure history but also philosophy of politics. The author sincerely hopes it will be interesting and bring new insights for interpreting both the past and contemporary reality.

Bibliography

Ukrainian Revolution

Hryn, H. (Ed.). (2005). The Ukrainian revolution, 1917-1921: A study in nationalism. Canadian Institute of Ukrainian Studies Press.

Katchanovski, I., Kohut, Z., Nebesio, B., & Yurkevich, M. (Eds.). (2019). Historical dictionary of Ukraine. Rowman & Littlefield.

Magocsi, P. R. (1996). A history of Ukraine. University of Toronto Press.

Subtelny, O. (2009). Ukraine: A history. University of Toronto Press.

Serhiichuk, V. (2017). The Ukrainian Revolution and the struggle for statehood, 1917-1920. Harvard Ukrainian Research Institute.

Contemporary Ukraine

Horbulin, V., & Libanova, E. (Eds.). (2019). Ukraine: The war's human face. Center for Army, Conversion, and Disarmament Studies.

Kuzio, T. (2015). Ukraine at the Crossroads: Economic Reforms and Challenges Ahead. Rowman & Littlefield.

Wilson, A. (2017). Ukraine Crisis: What it Means for the West. Yale University Press.

Zhurzhenko, T. (2019). War and Memory in Russia, Ukraine and Belarus. Palgrave Macmillan.

Contemporary Russia

Sakwa, R. (2019). Russia Against the Rest: The Post-Cold War Crisis of World Order. Cambridge University Press.

Galeotti, M. (2019). A Short History of Russia. Oxford University Press.

Arutunyan, A. (2018). The Putin Mystique: Inside Russia's Power Cult. Skyhorse Publishing.

Gessen, M. (2017). The Future is History: How Totalitarianism Reclaimed Russia. Riverhead Books.

McFaul, M. (2014). Russia's Unfinished Revolution: Political Change from Gorbachev to Putin. Cornell University Press.

Bolsheviks in Ukraine

Von Hagen, M. (1993). Soldiers in the Proletarian Dictatorship: The Red Army and the Soviet Socialist State, 1917-1930. Cornell University Press.

Mace, J. (2007). Communist Party Membership in the Bolshevik Revolution. Indiana University Press.

Kenez, P. (2015). Red Advance, White Defeat: Civil War in South Russia 1919-1920. Cambridge University Press.

Brovkin, V. N. (2013). Behind the Front Lines of the Civil War: Political Parties and Social Movements in Russia, 1918-1922. Princeton University Press.

Andreyev, C. (2007). Vlasov and the Russian Liberation Movement: Soviet Reality and Emigré Theories. Cambridge University Press.

Socialism and regional politics

Tismaneanu, V. (2014). The Devil in History: Communism, Fascism, and Some Lessons of the Twentieth Century. University of California Press.

Verdery, K. (1996). What Was Socialism, and What Comes Next?. Princeton University Press.

Sasse, G. (2008). The Crimea Question: Identity, Transition, and Conflict. Harvard University Press.

Mungiu-Pippidi, A. (2015). The Quest for Good Governance: How Societies Develop Control of Corruption. Cambridge University Press.

Lane, D. (2012). The Rise and Fall of State Socialism: Industrial Society and the Socialist State. Routledge.

Early communism in general

Service, R. (2011). Lenin: A Biography. Harvard University Press.

Read, C. (2005). Lenin: A Revolutionary Life. Routledge.

Volkogonov, D. (1994). Lenin: A New Biography. The Free Press.

Schapiro, L. (1970). The Origin of the Communist Autocracy: Political Opposition in the Soviet State First Phase 1917-1922.

Macmillan. Pipes, R. (1996). The Unknown Lenin: From the Secret Archive. Yale University Press.

Culture and politics

Wilson, A. (2015). Ukrainians in North America: A Biographical Directory of Noteworthy Men and Women of Ukrainian Origin in the United States and Canada. The Ukrainian Museum.

Magocsi, P. R. (2018). History of Ukraine: The Land and Its Peoples. University of Toronto Press.

Gorbachevych, O. (2019). Cultural Diplomacy of Ukraine: History and Modernity. The International Centre for Policy Studies.

Bilokin, S. (2016). The Ideological and Political Struggle for a New Ukrainian Statehood: Post-Soviet Political Landscape. Cambridge Scholars Publishing.

First World War

Holquist, P. (1992). Making War, Forging Revolution: Russia's Continuum of Crisis, 1914-1921. Harvard University Press.

Ohayon, I. (2017). The Great War in Russian Memory. Indiana University Press.

Portnov, A., & Wanner, C. (Eds.). (2017). Russian Postsoviet Puzzles: Mapping the Political Landscape. Routledge.

Decommunization

Kulyk, V. (2018). Decommunization and the Conceptual Change in Post-Soviet Ukraine. Central European University Press.

Verkhohliad, O. (2016). Decommunization and Decolonization in Ukraine: New Myths and Legitimation. Ibidem Press.

Bilinsky, Y. (2019). Endgame in NATO's Enlargement: The Baltic States and Ukraine. Purdue University Press.

Yekelchyk, S. (2015). The Conflict in Ukraine: What Everyone Needs to Know. Oxford University Press.

UKRAINIAN VOICES

Collected by Andreas Umland

1. *Mychailo Wynnyckyj*
   Ukraine's Maidan, Russia's War
   A Chronicle and Analysis of the Revolution of Dignity
   With a foreword by Serhii Plokhy
   ISBN 978-3-8382-1327-9

2. *Olexander Hryb*
   Understanding Contemporary Ukrainian and Russian Nationalism
   The Post-Soviet Cossack Revival and Ukraine's National Security
   With a foreword by Vitali Vitaliev
   ISBN 978-3-8382-1377-4

3. *Marko Bojcun*
   Towards a Political Economy of Ukraine
   Selected Essays 1990–2015
   With a foreword by John-Paul Himka
   ISBN 978-3-8382-1368-2

4. *Volodymyr Yermolenko (ed.)*
   Ukraine in Histories and Stories
   Essays by Ukrainian Intellectuals
   With a preface by Peter Pomerantsev
   ISBN 978-3-8382-1456-6

5. *Mykola Riabchuk*
   At the Fence of Metternich's Garden
   Essays on Europe, Ukraine, and Europeanization
   ISBN 978-3-8382-1484-9

6. *Marta Dyczok*
   Ukraine Calling
   A Kaleidoscope from Hromadske Radio 2016–2019
   With a foreword by Andriy Kulykov
   ISBN 978-3-8382-1472-6

7. *Olexander Scherba*
   Ukraine vs. Darkness
   Undiplomatic Thoughts
   With a foreword by Adrian Karatnycky
   ISBN 978-3-8382-1501-3

8. *Olesya Yaremchuk*
   Our Others
   Stories of Ukrainian Diversity
   With a foreword by Ostap Slyvynsky
   Translated from the Ukrainian by Zenia Tompkins and Hanna Leliv
   ISBN 978-3-8382-1475-7

9. *Nataliya Gumenyuk*
   Die verlorene Insel
   Geschichten von der besetzten Krim
   Mit einem Vorwort von Alice Bota
   Aus dem Ukrainischen übersetzt von Johann Zajaczkowski
   ISBN 978-3-8382-1499-3

10. *Olena Stiazhkina*
    Zero Point Ukraine
    Four Essays on World War II
    Translated from the Ukrainian by Svitlana Kulinska
    ISBN 978-3-8382-1550-1

11 Oleksii Sinchenko, Dmytro Stus, Leonid Finberg (compilers)
Ukrainian Dissidents
An Anthology of Texts
ISBN 978-3-8382-1551-8

12 John-Paul Himka
Ukrainian Nationalists and the Holocaust
OUN and UPA's Participation in the Destruction of Ukrainian Jewry, 1941–1944
ISBN 978-3-8382-1548-8

13 Andrey Demartino
False Mirrors
The Weaponization of Social Media in Russia's Operation to Annex Crimea
With a foreword by Oleksiy Danilov
ISBN 978-3-8382-1533-4

14 Svitlana Biedarieva (ed.)
Contemporary Ukrainian and Baltic Art
Political and Social Perspectives, 1991–2021
ISBN 978-3-8382-1526-6

15 Olesya Khromeychuk
A Loss
The Story of a Dead Soldier Told by His Sister
With a foreword by Andrey Kurkov
ISBN 978-3-8382-1570-9

16 Marieluise Beck (Hg.)
Ukraine verstehen
Auf den Spuren von Terror und Gewalt
Mit einem Vorwort von Dmytro Kuleba
ISBN 978-3-8382-1653-9

17 Stanislav Aseyev
Heller Weg
Geschichte eines Konzentrationslagers im Donbass 2017–2019
Aus dem Russischen übersetzt von Martina Steis und Charis Haska
ISBN 978-3-8382-1620-1

18 Mykola Davydiuk
Wie funktioniert Putins Propaganda?
Anmerkungen zum Informationskrieg des Kremls
Aus dem Ukrainischen übersetzt von Christian Weise
ISBN 978-3-8382-1628-7

19 Olesya Yaremchuk
Unsere Anderen
Geschichten ukrainischer Vielfalt
Aus dem Ukrainischen übersetzt von Christian Weise
ISBN 978-3-8382-1635-5

20 Oleksandr Mykhed
„Dein Blut wird die Kohle tränken"
Über die Ostukraine
Aus dem Ukrainischen übersetzt von Simon Muschick und Dario Planert
ISBN 978-3-8382-1648-5

21 Vakhtang Kipiani (Hg.)
Der Zweite Weltkrieg in der Ukraine
Geschichte und Lebensgeschichten
Aus dem Ukrainischen übersetzt von Margarita Grinko
ISBN 978-3-8382-1622-5

22 Vakhtang Kipiani (ed.)
World War II, Uncontrived and Unredacted
Testimonies from Ukraine
Translated from the Ukrainian by Zenia Tompkins and Daisy Gibbons
ISBN 978-3-8382-1621-8

23 Dmytro Stus
   Vasyl Stus
   Life in Creativity
   Translated from the Ukrainian by
   Ludmila Bachurina
   ISBN 978-3-8382-1631-7

24 Vitalii Ogiienko (ed.)
   The Holodomor and the
   Origins of the Soviet Man
   Reading the Testimony of
   Anastasia Lysyvets
   With forewords by Natalka
   Bilotserkivets and Serhy
   Yekelchyk
   Translated from the Ukrainian by
   Alla Parkhomenko and
   Alexander J. Motyl
   ISBN 978-3-8382-1616-4

25 Vladislav Davidzon
   Jewish-Ukrainian Relations
   and the Birth of a Political
   Nation
   Selected Writings 2013-2021
   With a foreword by Bernard-
   Henri Lévy
   ISBN 978-3-8382-1509-9

26 Serhy Yekelchyk
   Writing the Nation
   The Ukrainian Historical
   Profession in Independent
   Ukraine and the Diaspora
   ISBN 978-3-8382-1695-9

27 Ildi Eperjesi, Oleksandr
   Kachura
   Shreds of War
   Fates from the Donbas Frontline
   2014-2019
   With a foreword by Olexiy
   Haran
   ISBN 978-3-8382-1680-5

28 Oleksandr Melnyk
   World War II as an Identity
   Project
   Historicism, Legitimacy
   Contests, and the (Re-)Con-
   struction of Political Commu-
   nities in Ukraine, 1939–1946
   With a foreword by David R.
   Marples
   ISBN 978-3-8382-1704-8

29 Olesya Khromeychuk
   Ein Verlust
   Die Geschichte eines gefallenen
   ukrainischen Soldaten, erzählt
   von seiner Schwester
   Mit einem Vorwort von Andrej
   Kurkow
   Aus dem Englischen übersetzt
   von Lily Sophie
   ISBN 978-3-8382-1770-3

30 Tamara Martsenyuk,
   Tetiana Kostiuchenko (eds.)
   Russia's War in Ukraine
   During 2022
   Personal Experiences of
   Ukrainian Scholars
   ISBN 978-3-8382-1757-4

31 Ildikó Eperjesi, Oleksandr
   Kachura
   Shreds of War. Vol. 2
   Fates from Crimea 2015–2022
   With an interview of Oleh
   Sentsov
   ISBN 978-3-8382-1780-2

32 Yuriy Lukanov
   The Press
   How Russia Destroyed Media
   Freedom in Crimea
   With a foreword by Taras Kuzio
   ISBN 978-3-8382-1784-0

33 Megan Buskey
   Ukraine Is Not Dead Yet
   A Family Story of Exile and
   Return
   ISBN 978-3-8382-1691-1

34 Vira Ageyeva
Behind the Scenes of the
Empire
Essays on Cultural
Relationships between Ukraine
and Russia
With a foreword by Oksana
Zabuzhko
ISBN 978-3-8382-1748-2

35 Marieluise Beck (ed.)
Understanding Ukraine
Tracing the Roots of Terror and
Violence
With a foreword by Dmytro
Kuleba
ISBN 978-3-8382-1773-4

36 Olesya Khromeychuk
A Loss
The Story of a Dead Soldier Told
by His Sister, 2nd edn.
With a foreword by Philippe
Sands
With a preface by Andrii Kurkov
ISBN 978-3-8382-1870-0

37 Taras Kuzio, Stefan
Jajecznyk-Kelman
Fascism and Genocide
Russia's War Against
Ukrainians
ISBN 978-3-8382-1791-8

38 Alina Nychyk
Ukraine Vis-à-Vis Russia
and the EU
Misperceptions of Foreign
Challenges in Times of War,
2014–2015
With a foreword by Paul
D'Anieri
ISBN 978-3-8382-1767-3

39 Sasha Dovzhyk (ed.)
Ukraine Lab
Global Security, Environment,
and Disinformation Through the
Prism of Ukraine
With a foreword by Rory Finnin
ISBN 978-3-8382-1805-2

40 Serhiy Kvit
Media, History, and
Education
Three Ways to Ukrainian
Independence
With a preface by Diane Francis
ISBN 978-3-8382-1807-6

41 Anna Romandash
Women of Ukraine
Reportages from the War and
Beyond
ISBN 978-3-8382-1819-9

42 Dominika Rank
Matzewe in meinem Garten
Abenteuer eines jüdischen
Heritage-Touristen in der
Ukraine
ISBN 978-3-8382-1810-6

43 Myroslaw Marynowytsch
Das Universum hinter dem
Stacheldraht
Memoiren eines sowjet-
ukrainischen Dissidenten
Mit einem Vorwort von Timothy
Snyder und einem Nachwort
von Max Hartmann
ISBN 978-3-8382-1806-9

44 Konstantin Sigow
Für Deine und meine
Freiheit
Europäische Revolutions- und
Kriegserfahrungen im heutigen
Kyjiw
Mit einem Vorwort von Karl
Schlögel
Herausgegeben von Regula M.
Zwahlen
ISBN 978-3-8382-1755-0

45 Kateryna Pylypchuk
The War that Changed Us
Ukrainian Novellas, Poems, and
Essays from 2022
With a foreword by Victor
Yushchenko
Paperback
ISBN 978-3-8382-1859-5
Hardcover
ISBN 978-3-8382-1860-1

46 Kyrylo Tkachenko
Rechte Tür Links
Radikale Linke in Deutschland, die Revolution und der Krieg in der Ukraine, 2013-2018
ISBN 978-3-8382-1711-6

47 Alexander Strashny
The Ukrainian Mentality
An Ethno-Psychological, Historical and Comparative Exploration
With a foreword by Antonina Lovochkina
Translated from the Ukrainian by Michael M. Naydan and Olha Tytarenko
ISBN 978-3-8382-1886-1

48 Alona Shestopalova
From Screens to Battlefields
Tracing the Construction of Enemies on Russian Television
With a foreword by Nina Jankowicz
ISBN 978-3-8382-1884-7

49 Iaroslav Petik
Politics and Society in the Ukrainian People's Republic (1917–1921) and Contemporary Ukraine (2013–2022)
A Comparative Analysis
With a foreword by Mykola Doroshko
ISBN 978-3-8382-1817-5

50 Serhii Plokhy
Der Mann mit der Giftpistole
Eine Spionagegeschichte aus dem Kalten Krieg
ISBN 978-3-8382-1789-5

51 Vakhtang Kipiani
Ukrainische Dissidenten unter der Sowjetmacht
Im Kampf um Wahrheit und Freiheit
Aus dem Ukrainischen übersetzt von Christian Weise
ISBN 978-3-8382-1890-8

52 Dmytro Shestakov
When Businesses Test Hypotheses
A Four-Step Approach to Risk Management for Innovative Startups
With a foreword by Anthony J. Tether
ISBN 978-3-8382-1883-0

53 Larissa Babij
A Kind of Refugee
The Story of an American Who Refused to Leave Ukraine
With a foreword by Vladislav Davidzon
ISBN 978-3-8382-1898-4

54 Julia Davis
In Their Own Words
How Russian Propagandists Reveal Putin's Intentions
With a foreword by Timothy Snyder
ISBN 978-3-8382-1909-7

55 Sonya Atlantova, Oleksandr Klymenko
Icons on Ammo Boxes
Painting Life on the Remnants of Russia's War in Donbas, 2014-21
Translated from the Ukrainian by Anastasya Knyazhytska
ISBN 978-3-8382-1892-2

56 Leonid Ushkalov
Catching an Elusive Bird
The Life of Hryhorii Skovoroda
Translated from the Ukrainian by Natalia Komarova
ISBN 978-3-8382-1894-6

57 Vakhtang Kipiani
Ein Land weiblichen Geschlechts
Ukrainische Frauenschicksale im 20. und 21. Jahrhundert
Aus dem Ukrainischen übersetzt von Christian Weise
ISBN 978-3-8382-1891-5

58 Petro Rychlo
„Zerrissne Saiten einer überlauten Harfe ..."
Deutschjüdische Dichter der Bukowina
ISBN 978-3-8382-1893-9

59 Volodymyr Paniotto
Sociology in Jokes
An Entertaining Introduction
ISBN 978-3-8382-1857-1

60 Josef Wallmannsberger (ed.)
Executing Renaissances
The Poetological Nation of Ukraine
ISBN 978-3-8382-1741-3

61 Pavlo Kazarin
The Wild West of Eastern Europe
ISBN 978-3-8382-1842-7

62 Ernest Gyidel
Ukrainian Public Nationalism in the General Government
The Case of Krakivski Visti, 1940–1944
With a foreword by David R. Marples
ISBN 978-3-8382-1865-6

63 Olexander Hryb
Understanding Contemporary Russian Militarism
From Revolutionary to New Generation Warfare
With a foreword by Mark Laity
ISBN 978-3-8382-1927-1

64 Orysia Hrudka, Bohdan Ben
Dark Days, Determined People
Stories from Ukraine under Siege
With a foreword by Myroslav Marynovych
ISBN 978-3-8382-1958-5

65 Oleksandr Pankieiev (ed.)
Narratives of the Russo-Ukrainian War
A Look Within and Without
With a foreword by Natalia Khanenko-Friesen
ISBN 978-3-8382-1964-6

66 Roman Sohn, Ariana Gic (eds.)
Unrecognized War
The Fight for Truth about Russia's War on Ukraine
With a foreword by Viktor Yushchenko
ISBN 978-3-8382-1947-9

67 Paul Robert Magocsi
Ukraina Redux
Schon wieder die Ukraine ...
ISBN 978-3-8382-1942-4

68 Paul Robert Magocsi
L'Ucraina Ritrovata
Sullo Stato e l'Identità Nazionale
ISBN 978-3-8382-1982-0

Book series "Ukrainian Voices"

Coordinator
Andreas Umland, National University of Kyiv-Mohyla Academy

Editorial Board
Lesia Bidochko, National University of Kyiv-Mohyla Academy
Svitlana Biedarieva, George Washington University, DC, USA
Ivan Gomza, Kyiv School of Economics, Ukraine
Natalie Jaresko, Aspen Institute, Kyiv/Washington
Olena Lennon, University of New Haven, West Haven, USA
Kateryna Yushchenko, First Lady of Ukraine 2005-2010, Kyiv
Oleksandr Zabirko, University of Regensburg, Germany

Advisory Board
Iuliia Bentia, National Academy of Arts of Ukraine, Kyiv
Natalya Belitser, Pylyp Orlyk Institute for Democracy, Kyiv
Oleksandra Bienert, Humboldt University of Berlin, Germany
Sergiy Bilenky, Canadian Institute of Ukrainian Studies, Toronto
Tymofii Brik, Kyiv School of Economics, Ukraine
Olga Brusylovska, Mechnikov National University, Odesa
Mariana Budjeryn, Harvard University, Cambridge, USA
Volodymyr Bugrov, Shevchenko National University, Kyiv
Olga Burlyuk, University of Amsterdam, The Netherlands
Yevhen Bystrytsky, NAS Institute of Philosophy, Kyiv
Andrii Danylenko, Pace University, New York, USA
Vladislav Davidzon, Atlantic Council, Washington/Paris
Mykola Davydiuk, Think Tank "Polityka," Kyiv
Andrii Demartino, National Security and Defense Council, Kyiv
Vadym Denisenko, Ukrainian Institute for the Future, Kyiv
Oleksandr Donii, Center for Political Values Studies, Kyiv
Volodymyr Dubovyk, Mechnikov National University, Odesa
Volodymyr Dubrovskiy, CASE Ukraine, Kyiv
Diana Dutsyk, National University of Kyiv-Mohyla Academy
Marta Dyczok, Western University, Ontario, Canada
Yevhen Fedchenko, National University of Kyiv-Mohyla Academy
Sofiya Filonenko, State Pedagogical University of Berdyansk
Oleksandr Fisun, Karazin National University, Kharkiv
Oksana Forostyna, Webjournal "Ukraina Moderna," Kyiv
Roman Goncharenko, Broadcaster "Deutsche Welle," Bonn
George Grabowicz, Harvard University, Cambridge, USA
Gelinada Grinchenko, Karazin National University, Kharkiv
Kateryna Härtel, Federal Union of European Nationalities, Brussels
Nataliia Hendel, University of Geneva, Switzerland
Anton Herashchenko, Kyiv School of Public Administration
John-Paul Himka, University of Alberta, Edmonton
Ola Hnatiuk, National University of Kyiv-Mohyla Academy
Oleksandr Holubov, Broadcaster "Deutsche Welle," Bonn
Yaroslav Hrytsak, Ukrainian Catholic University, Lviv
Oleksandra Humenna, National University of Kyiv-Mohyla Academy
Tamara Hundorova, NAS Institute of Literature, Kyiv
Oksana Huss, University of Bologna, Italy
Oleksandra Iwaniuk, University of Warsaw, Poland
Mykola Kapitonenko, Shevchenko National University, Kyiv
Georgiy Kasianov, Marie Curie-Skłodowska University, Lublin
Vakhtang Kebuladze, Shevchenko National University, Kyiv
Natalia Khanenko-Friesen, University of Alberta, Edmonton
Victoria Khiterer, Millersville University of Pennsylvania, USA
Oksana Kis, NAS Institute of Ethnology, Lviv
Pavlo Klimkin, Center for National Resilience and Development, Kyiv
Oleksandra Kolomiiets, Center for Economic Strategy, Kyiv

Sergiy Korsunsky, Kobe Gakuin University, Japan
Nadiia Koval, Kyiv School of Economics, Ukraine
Volodymyr Kravchenko, University of Alberta, Edmonton
Oleksiy Kresin, NAS Koretskiy Institute of State and Law, Kyiv
Anatoliy Kruglashov, Fedkovych National University, Chernivtsi
Andrey Kurkov, PEN Ukraine, Kyiv
Ostap Kushnir, Lazarski University, Warsaw
Taras Kuzio, National University of Kyiv-Mohyla Academy
Serhii Kvit, National University of Kyiv-Mohyla Academy
Yuliya Ladygina, The Pennsylvania State University, USA
Yevhen Mahda, Institute of World Policy, Kyiv
Victoria Malko, California State University, Fresno, USA
Yulia Marushevska, Security and Defense Center (SAND), Kyiv
Myroslav Marynovych, Ukrainian Catholic University, Lviv
Oleksandra Matviichuk, Center for Civil Liberties, Kyiv
Mykhailo Minakov, Kennan Institute, Washington, USA
Anton Moiseienko, The Australian National University, Canberra
Alexander Motyl, Rutgers University-Newark, USA
Vlad Mykhnenko, University of Oxford, United Kingdom
Vitalii Ogiienko, Ukrainian Institute of National Remembrance, Kyiv
Olga Onuch, University of Manchester, United Kingdom
Olesya Ostrovska, Museum "Mystetskyi Arsenal," Kyiv
Anna Osypchuk, National University of Kyiv-Mohyla Academy
Oleksandr Pankieiev, University of Alberta, Edmonton
Oleksiy Panych, Publishing House "Dukh i Litera," Kyiv
Valerii Pekar, Kyiv-Mohyla Business School, Ukraine
Yohanan Petrovsky-Shtern, Northwestern University, Chicago
Serhii Plokhy, Harvard University, Cambridge, USA
Andrii Portnov, Viadrina University, Frankfurt-Oder, Germany
Maryna Rabinovych, Kyiv School of Economics, Ukraine
Valentyna Romanova, Institute of Developing Economies, Tokyo
Natalya Ryabinska, Collegium Civitas, Warsaw, Poland

Darya Tsymbalyk, University of Oxford, United Kingdom
Vsevolod Samokhvalov, University of Liege, Belgium
Orest Semotiuk, Franko National University, Lviv
Viktoriya Sereda, NAS Institute of Ethnology, Lviv
Anton Shekhovtsov, University of Vienna, Austria
Andriy Shevchenko, Media Center Ukraine, Kyiv
Oxana Shevel, Tufts University, Medford, USA
Pavlo Shopin, National Pedagogical Dragomanov University, Kyiv
Karina Shyrokykh, Stockholm University, Sweden
Nadja Simon, freelance interpreter, Cologne, Germany
Olena Snigova, NAS Institute for Economics and Forecasting, Kyiv
Ilona Solohub, Analytical Platform "VoxUkraine," Kyiv
Iryna Solonenko, LibMod - Center for Liberal Modernity, Berlin
Galyna Solovei, National University of Kyiv-Mohyla Academy
Sergiy Stelmakh, NAS Institute of World History, Kyiv
Olena Stiazhkina, NAS Institute of the History of Ukraine, Kyiv
Dmitri Stratievski, Osteuropa Zentrum (OEZB), Berlin
Dmytro Stus, National Taras Shevchenko Museum, Kyiv
Frank Sysyn, University of Toronto, Canada
Olha Tokariuk, Center for European Policy Analysis, Washington
Olena Tregub, Independent Anti-Corruption Commission, Kyiv
Hlib Vyshlinsky, Centre for Economic Strategy, Kyiv
Mychailo Wynnyckyj, National University of Kyiv-Mohyla Academy
Yelyzaveta Yasko, NGO "Yellow Blue Strategy," Kyiv
Serhy Yekelchyk, University of Victoria, Canada
Victor Yushchenko, President of Ukraine 2005-2010, Kyiv
Oleksandr Zaitsev, Ukrainian Catholic University, Lviv
Kateryna Zarembo, National University of Kyiv-Mohyla Academy
Yaroslav Zhalilo, National Institute for Strategic Studies, Kyiv
Sergei Zhuk, Ball State University at Muncie, USA
Alina Zubkovych, Nordic Ukraine Forum, Stockholm
Liudmyla Zubrytska, National University of Kyiv-Mohyla Academy

Friends of the Series

Ana Maria Abulescu, University of Bucharest, Romania
Łukasz Adamski, Centrum Mieroszewskiego, Warsaw
Marieluise Beck, LibMod—Center for Liberal Modernity, Berlin
Marc Berensen, King's College London, United Kingdom
Johannes Bohnen, BOHNEN Public Affairs, Berlin
Karsten Brüggemann, University of Tallinn, Estonia
Ulf Brunnbauer, Leibniz Institute (IOS), Regensburg
Martin Dietze, German-Ukrainian Culture Society, Hamburg
Gergana Dimova, Florida State University, Tallahassee/London
Caroline von Gall, Goethe University, Frankfurt-Main
Zaur Gasimov, Rhenish Friedrich Wilhelm University, Bonn
Armand Gosu, University of Bucharest, Romania
Thomas Grant, University of Cambridge, United Kingdom
Gustav Gressel, European Council on Foreign Relations, Berlin
Rebecca Harms, European Centre for Press & Media Freedom, Leipzig
André Härtel, Stiftung Wissenschaft und Politik, Berlin/Brussels
Marcel Van Herpen, The Cicero Foundation, Maastricht
Richard Herzinger, freelance analyst, Berlin
Mieste Hotopp-Riecke, ICATAT, Magdeburg
Nico Lange, Munich Security Conference, Berlin
Martin Malek, freelance analyst, Vienna
Ingo Mannteufel, Broadcaster "Deutsche Welle," Bonn
Carlo Masala, Bundeswehr University, Munich
Wolfgang Mueller, University of Vienna, Austria
Dietmar Neutatz, Albert Ludwigs University, Freiburg
Torsten Oppelland, Friedrich Schiller University, Jena
Niccolò Pianciola, University of Padua, Italy
Gerald Praschl, German-Ukrainian Forum (DUF), Berlin
Felix Riefer, Think Tank Ideenagentur-Ost, Düsseldorf
Stefan Rohdewald, University of Leipzig, Germany
Sebastian Schäffer, Institute for the Danube Region (IDM), Vienna
Felix Schimansky-Geier, Friedrich Schiller University, Jena
Ulrich Schneckener, University of Osnabrück, Germany

Winfried Schneider-Deters, freelance analyst, Heidelberg/Kyiv
Gerhard Simon, University of Cologne, Germany
Kai Struve, Martin Luther University, Halle/Wittenberg
David Stulik, European Values Center for Security Policy, Prague
Andrzej Szeptycki, University of Warsaw, Poland
Philipp Ther, University of Vienna, Austria
Stefan Troebst, University of Leipzig, Germany

[Please send address requests for changes, corrections, and additions to this list to andreas.umland@stanforalumni.org.]

ibidem.eu